Presented to

_____

With love from

_____

Date

_____

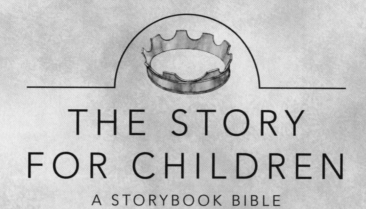

THE STORY
FOR CHILDREN

A STORYBOOK BIBLE

For our grandchildren—

*"Write these things for the future so that people
who are not yet born will praise the Lord."*

Psalm 102:18 (NCV)

—The Authors

THE STORY
FOR CHILDREN

A STORYBOOK BIBLE

Written by

MAX LUCADO, RANDY FRAZEE, AND KAREN DAVIS HILL

Illustrated by

FAUSTO BIANCHI

ZONDERkidz

ZONDERVAN.com/
AUTHORTRACKER
follow your favorite author

ZONDERKIDZ

The Story for Children
Copyright © 2011 by Max Lucado, Randy Frazee, and Karen Davis Hill
Illustrations © 2011 by Fausto Bianchi

Requests for information should be addressed to:

Zondervan, *Grand Rapids, Michigan 49530*

Library of Congress Cataloging-in-Publication Data

The Story for children : a storybook bible /written by Max Lucado with Karen
Davis Hill and Randy Frazee ; illustrated by Fausto Bianchi.
    p.   cm.
ISBN 978-0-310-71975-5 (hardcover)
1. Bible stories, English. I. Hill, Karen, 1947- II. Frazee, Randy. III. Bianchi, Fausto.
Iv. Title.
BS551.3.L83 2011
220.9'505—dc22   2011014460

Editors: Barbara Herndon and Doris Rikkers
Art direction and design: Kris Nelson
Illustrator: Fausto Bianchi, represented by Beehive Illustration
Artwork colorist: Steve James

Printed in the United States of America

11 12 13 14 /DWO/ 22 21 20 19 18 17 16 15 14 13 12 11 10 9 8 7 6 5 4 3 2 1

A word from the authors …

When our children are young, we secure them with seat belts and snap them into swim vests. We schedule regular checkups, show them how to floss, and make sure they get plenty of rest. We teach them right from wrong, urge caution when crossing the street. Our job? Their safety and well-being. We want our children to live healthy, full lives.

When it comes to our children's eternal lives, we guide them to the anchor of our faith: God's Word. We fill their young spirits with the stories of old: faithful Abraham, courageous Daniel, lyrical David, obedient Mary.

We do what generations of parents before us have done: pass down to our children the legacy of God's Holy Word. In this collection of great Bible stories, we continue that tradition, while adding some interpretive thoughts to help children grasp God's grand plan for their own lives. Our goal? To show that each one of us has a unique place in a much larger story. We want your children to see that Scripture is more than a collection of fascinating characters, thrilling adventures, and dramatic encounters. We want them to accept God's purpose in creating them, his desire to reunite with them, and his incomparable, amazing love for them.

Our prayer is that these stories will compel your child's fascination with Scripture, lay a foundation for a life of faith, and remind them: "The word of God is living and active …" Hebrews 4:12 (NIrV).

In the meantime, keep buckling, snapping, flossing … and most of all keep praying for the little souls in your care.

Max Lucado   Randy Frazee   Karen Hill

Table of Contents

Chapter 1

The Beginning of Life as We Know It

In the beginning,
God created the heavens and the earth.

Genesis 1:1

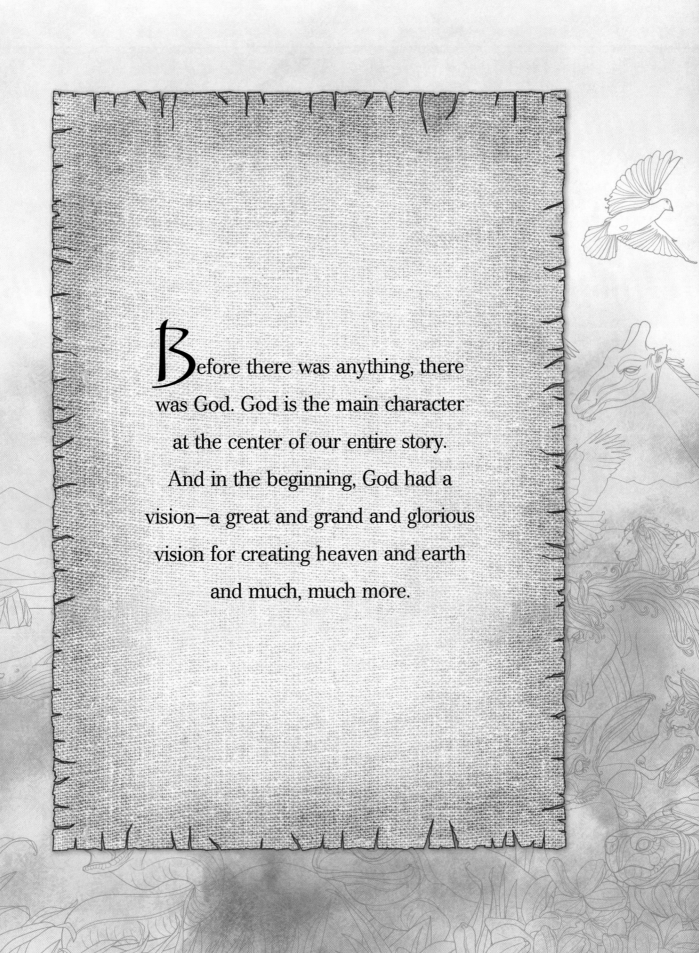

Before there was anything, there was God. God is the main character at the center of our entire story. And in the beginning, God had a vision—a great and grand and glorious vision for creating heaven and earth and much, much more.

The Creation

Genesis 1–2

With sweeping brush strokes, God painted his creation across the emptiness.

"Let there be light," he called into the darkness, and a sweep of brightness blazed across the blank canvas. He called the light "day," and the darkness he called "night." That was day one.

On day two, God called out into the light, "Let there be space between the water above and the water below." He called this big blue area "sky."

"Let the water gather in one place so land will appear," God commanded on day three. And it was so.

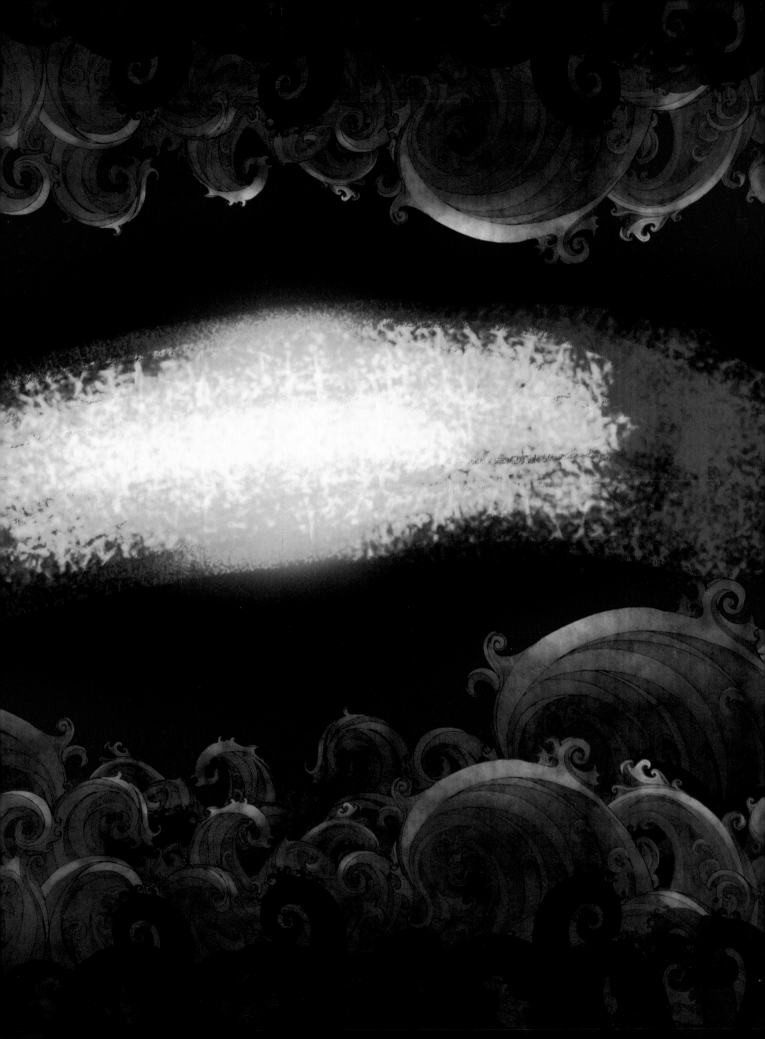

Then God said, "Let the land produce plants and trees bearing fruit." And the sweet smell of lilacs and apple blossoms filled the air.

On day four, God said, "Let the sun shine on the earth to mark the day, and let the moon and the sparkling stars mark the night." And it happened.

Then, on day five, God said, "Let creatures fill the oceans and rivers, the lakes and the streams. Let birds fly high in the sky." And sunfish and porpoises splashed in the waves, while eagles and robins soared above them.

14

On the sixth day, God said, "Let living creatures roam the earth." And animals of every shape and size and color appeared.

Then God stepped back, pleased with his creation. And it was all very good.

But something was missing. God made the earth, the sky, and everything in it, but this was not God's entire plan. He was not finished. The best was yet to come.

On this same day, God did his finest work. He created people in his own image. God created a man named Adam and a woman named Eve. He now had a part of creation that he could have a close and loving relationship with.

Then God stepped back, took a look, and said, "This is very, very good!"

God's Message

You are my greatest creation.

Looking at you is better than looking at an ocean view.

Watching you run and play is better than watching beautiful animals dart across the African plain.

Seeing a smile on your face is better than seeing a sunrise.

You are my pride and joy.

God's Children Make a Choice

Genesis 2-3

Life in God's beautiful garden was off to a great start. Adam and Eve made themselves right at home hiking trails, splashing in clear streams, and racing across green fields.

Adam and Eve spent their days watching the animals romping and roaming around their new playground and spent cool evenings counting stars. At bedtime, they drifted into dreams as larks sang them to sleep.

Life was good in God's perfect world.

The food in God's garden was plentiful. After all the hiking, swimming, and climbing, Adam and Eve were hungry. God showed them the delicious buffet awaiting them: crispy-sweet carrots, mouth-watering mangoes, crunchy nuts, and plump berries.

But when Adam reached for the fruit in the center of the garden, God spoke up. "Anything but that one, Adam. That fruit from the tree of knowledge of good and evil is not for you to eat."

So Adam and Eve obeyed . . . for a while. But one day, a sneaky snake enticed Eve to try the forbidden fruit. "Try this—it's the best in the garden! One little bite won't hurt." So Eve plucked a piece and took a bite, then gave some to Adam.

When God found Adam and Eve hiding in the bushes, he knew they had disobeyed.

"I will always love you," God said. "But since you disobeyed me, you cannot live in this beautiful garden anymore."

Adam and Eve were sorry they could no longer be with God in his garden. They left with heavy hearts. But they were thankful they had not lost the most important thing of all— their heavenly Father's love.

God's Message

My heart aches knowing that we are separated by sin. But I will always love you.

I long for our talks in the cool of the evening.

I dream of our walks together in the garden.

We are separated now, but we won't be apart forever.

I promise one day we will be close again.

One Good Man Deserves a Fresh Start

Genesis 6–9

Many years passed. Adam and Eve had children who had more children who had more children. Soon, there were people all over the world. But they turned into selfish and greedy people. None of them cared about God. No one, that is, except Noah. Noah was a good man who loved God.

God made a plan to start all over with Noah.

"Noah, because you love me, I will save you and your family. But you have to do your part. Go and build an ark—a huge boat. Collect animals of every kind and food to feed them all. Take your wife, your sons, and their wives too. Then watch and wait. I will send water from heaven and water from the deep parts of the earth to cover the entire world. The flood will wipe out everything, but you will be safe inside the ark."

Noah believed God and obeyed him. Noah built the huge boat and marched the animals into the ark—every bird and beast and creeping thing: panda bears and pythons, camels and chameleons, elephants and egrets. When the animals were in place in the ark and Noah and his family were settled in their new home, God closed the door and sealed it shut.

Then God opened the windows of heaven and rain poured down out of the sky. The lakes, rivers, streams, and oceans surged over their banks. As the fountains of the deep poured over the earth, the water rose and the land and mountains disappeared. Days, weeks, and months passed. Noah and his family lived on the ark for more than forty days and forty nights waiting for God's signal that it was safe to leave.

First it stopped raining. Then the water began to go down. Noah released birds out of the ark to see if they could find a place to rest. When he sent out a dove for the third time, the bird did not return. This meant the dove had found a dry place to live.

It was a great day when Noah and his family and all the animals joyfully left the ark to live on the earth again.

God's Message

You have weathered a great storm.

I promise I will never again send a flood to cover the earth.

Look up at the sky. That rainbow is a sign of my promise.

It is a symbol of a fresh beginning between me and you and the whole world.

27

Chapter 2

God Builds a New Nation

"I will make you into a great nation.
I will bless you.
I will make your name great.
You will be a blessing to others."

Genesis 12:2

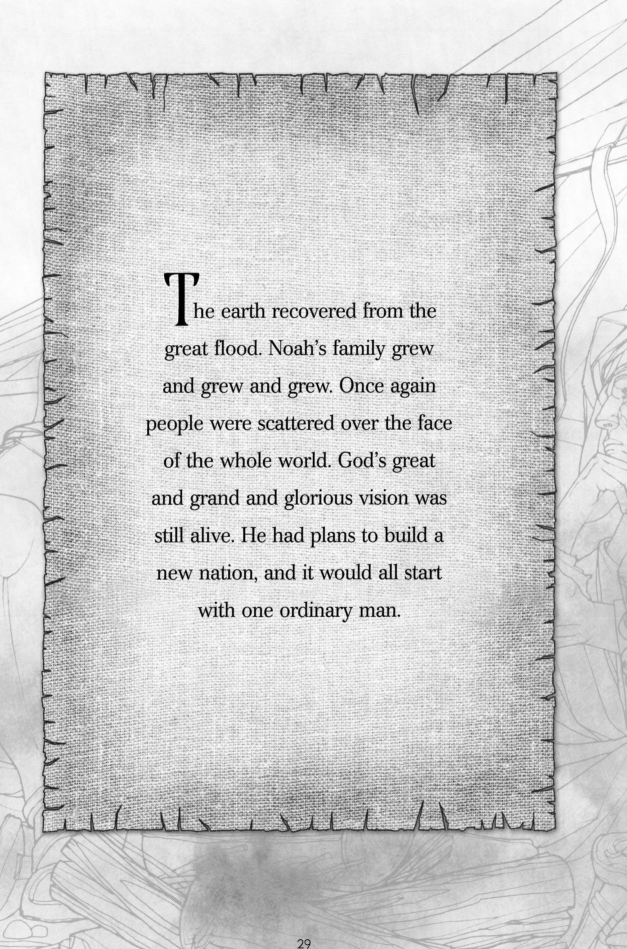

The earth recovered from the great flood. Noah's family grew and grew and grew. Once again people were scattered over the face of the whole world. God's great and grand and glorious vision was still alive. He had plans to build a new nation, and it would all start with one ordinary man.

Abraham Trusts God

Genesis 12:1–9; 15:1–6; 21:1–7

One day, God spoke to Abram, "I have big plans for you, Abram. I will bless you and make your name great. You will be a blessing to others. I will make you the father of a great nation. Leave your country and your people and go to a land I will show you. Pick up everything and start walking. Eventually I will show you where to stop."

Amazingly, Abram trusted God. He gathered the members of his household, packed up all his belongings, and started walking across the desert. He had no idea where he was going. When he arrived in the land of Canaan, God said, "You can stop walking, Abram. This is the land I am going to give you and all the people who come after you." So Abram and his wife Sarai pitched their tents and settled in the land.

Many years passed. Then one cool, dark night, God called to Abram in his tent. "Abram, come outside. Look up at the sky. Count the stars, if you can even count that high. I promise you will have as many children as there are stars in the heavens!"

Abram believed God. Even though Abram was old, even though his wife Sarai was old and had never been pregnant, Abram still believed God would make him into a great nation.

Many, many more years passed. Now Abram was 99 years old and Sarai was 90. Once again God spoke to Abram. "Abram, today I am making a covenant with you. You will be the father of many nations. Your name will now be Abraham. Give your wife the name Sarah, for she will be the mother of many nations. She soon will have a son."

Abraham fell on the ground, laughing. He said to himself, "A great nation will come from me? But how? Sarah and I are too old to have children!"

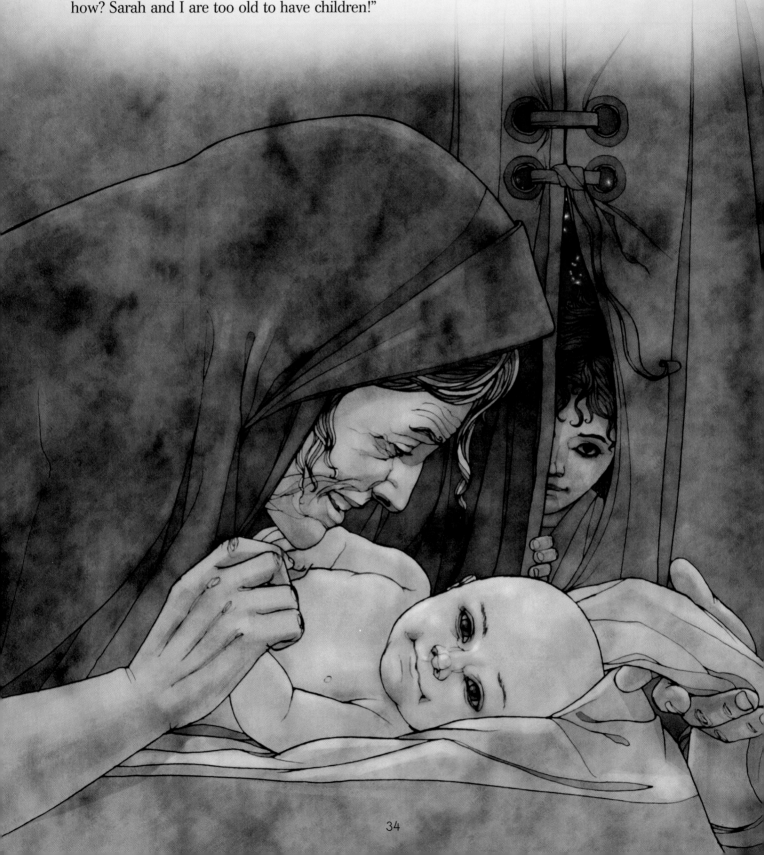

But soon Abraham and Sarah learned that nothing was too hard for God. A year later Sarah gave birth to a baby boy. Abraham named him Isaac (which means "to laugh").

When Isaac grew up, he married and had two sons: Esau and Jacob. Esau had five sons, and Jacob had twelve! Abraham's children would multiply like the stars in the heavens—just like God had promised.

God's Message

I will be your God forever and ever.

You and your relatives will be my special people.

My blessing will be with you and your children and your children's children through a thousand generations.

Chapter 3

Joseph: From Slave to Deputy Pharaoh

We know that in all things God works for the good of those who love him. He appointed them to be saved in keeping with his purpose.

Romans 8:28

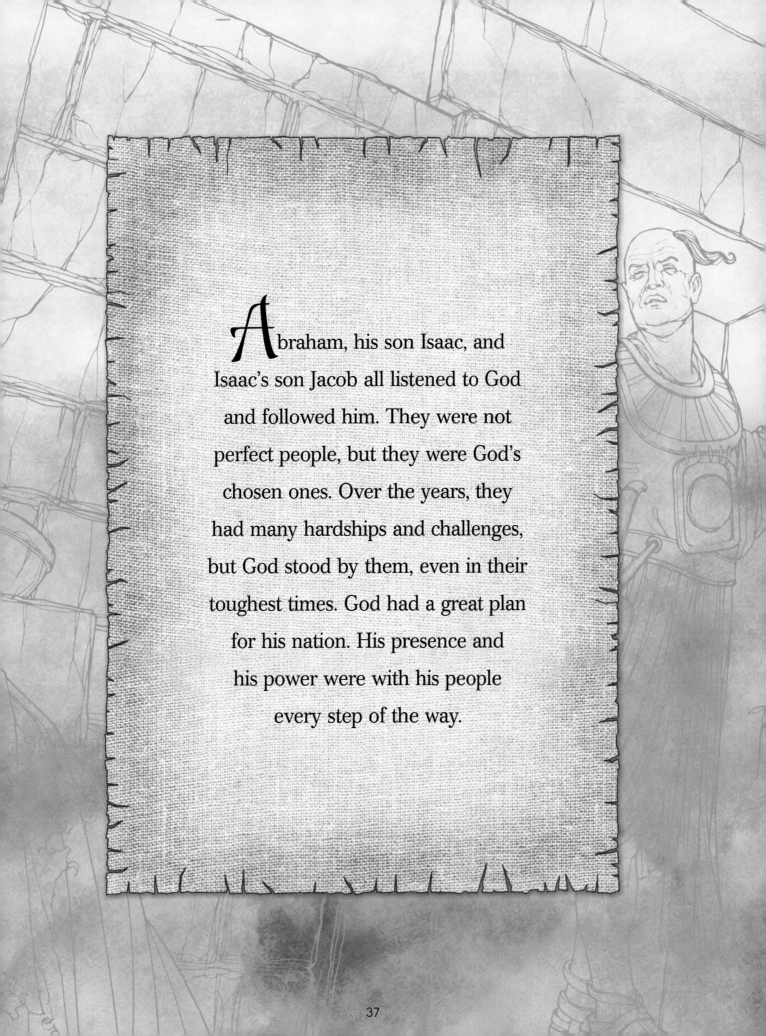

Abraham, his son Isaac, and Isaac's son Jacob all listened to God and followed him. They were not perfect people, but they were God's chosen ones. Over the years, they had many hardships and challenges, but God stood by them, even in their toughest times. God had a great plan for his nation. His presence and his power were with his people every step of the way.

The Favorite Son

Genesis 37

When Abraham's grandson Jacob grew up, he had many sons. But Jacob loved one son more than all the others: his son Joseph. To show his love for Joseph, Jacob made him a special gift—a beautiful coat of many colors. This made Joseph's brothers very jealous. They didn't like their father playing favorites.

"Listen to the dream I had," Joseph told his brothers one morning. "We were binding sheaves of grain when suddenly my sheaf stood straight up. Then your sheaves gathered around mine and bowed down to it."

Joseph's brothers were annoyed at the story. "Are you saying that WE will bow down to YOU someday?" The brothers grew even angrier.

Then, one day, Jacob sent Joseph out to visit his brothers who were in the fields tending the sheep. When they noticed Joseph coming, they saw a chance to get rid of the younger brother they hated so much.

The brothers grabbed Joseph, ripped off his beautiful coat, and threw him into a dry well. Soon, a caravan of camels and merchants came by on its way to Egypt.

"I've got an idea," said one of the brothers. "Let's sell Joseph to these men!" The brothers took Joseph out of the well and sold him to the merchants for 20 shekels of silver. Then they grabbed his coat, dipped it in animal blood, and took it to their father.

"Father," they cried, "look what we found!"

Jacob knew the robe belonged to Joseph. Jacob was heartbroken, believing the boy he loved so much was dead. For many days, Jacob mourned and wept for his son.

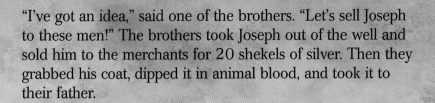

God's Message

When you feel your
heart is broken,
I will dry your tears.

When you feel afraid,
I will whisper words
of courage in your ear.

No matter where you go,
I am with you.

Nothing can separate
you from my love.

I am your God and
you are my child.

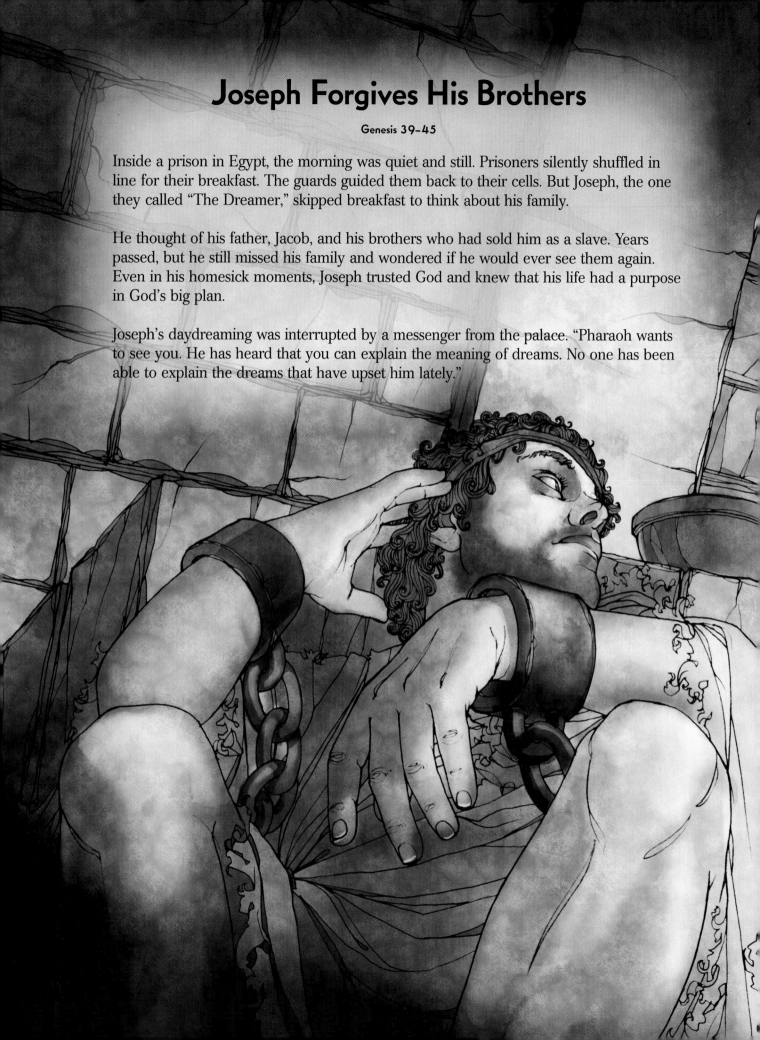

Joseph Forgives His Brothers

Genesis 39–45

Inside a prison in Egypt, the morning was quiet and still. Prisoners silently shuffled in line for their breakfast. The guards guided them back to their cells. But Joseph, the one they called "The Dreamer," skipped breakfast to think about his family.

He thought of his father, Jacob, and his brothers who had sold him as a slave. Years passed, but he still missed his family and wondered if he would ever see them again. Even in his homesick moments, Joseph trusted God and knew that his life had a purpose in God's big plan.

Joseph's daydreaming was interrupted by a messenger from the palace. "Pharaoh wants to see you. He has heard that you can explain the meaning of dreams. No one has been able to explain the dreams that have upset him lately."

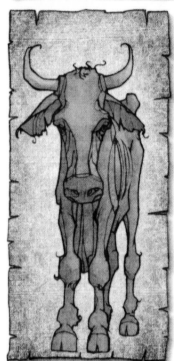

Joseph was taken to the palace. The king described his dreams of fat cows and skinny cows. "These dreams are keeping me awake," said Pharaoh.

Joseph told the king, "Only God has the power to explain dreams, but I trust him to help me understand." Joseph told Pharaoh the dreams were a warning of a terrible drought. "For years, no rain will come to the land. Without water, the crops will die. God is telling you to save food for your people. It is time to prepare," said Joseph.

Pharaoh believed Joseph. He said, "I will put you in charge of all these preparations, because I know God is with you."

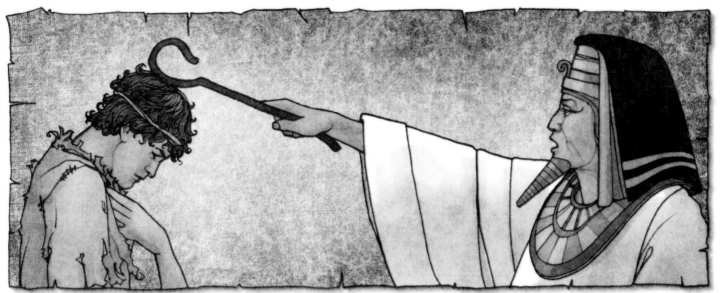

The people of Egypt followed Joseph's instructions, so when the drought came, they had plenty to eat. Other countries weren't prepared and ran out of food. Many people came to Egypt hungry. One day Joseph's own brothers came asking for food. It had been such a long time since they had seen Joseph, they didn't know who he was. But Joseph recognized his brothers.

Joseph made a special dinner for his brothers and gave them food to take back to their families. The brothers couldn't understand why this important man was being so kind to them.

Joseph watched them and waited, trying to decide what to do.

Finally he said, "I am your brother Joseph."

The brothers could hardly believe it. They were ashamed and afraid because of the way they had treated their little brother so long ago.

Joseph hugged his brothers. "Don't be mad at yourselves for what you did to me," he said. "Even though you meant to do something bad, God used your actions to do something good."

Joseph always knew God was with him. Now his life's journey made sense.

Soon the whole family gathered in Egypt. God did this good thing. Joseph and his family praised God for bringing them together again.

God's Message

The power of forgiveness has restored your family.

They will not just survive in this strange land, they will thrive here.

Always remember that when you trust me with your life, I will do great things through you.

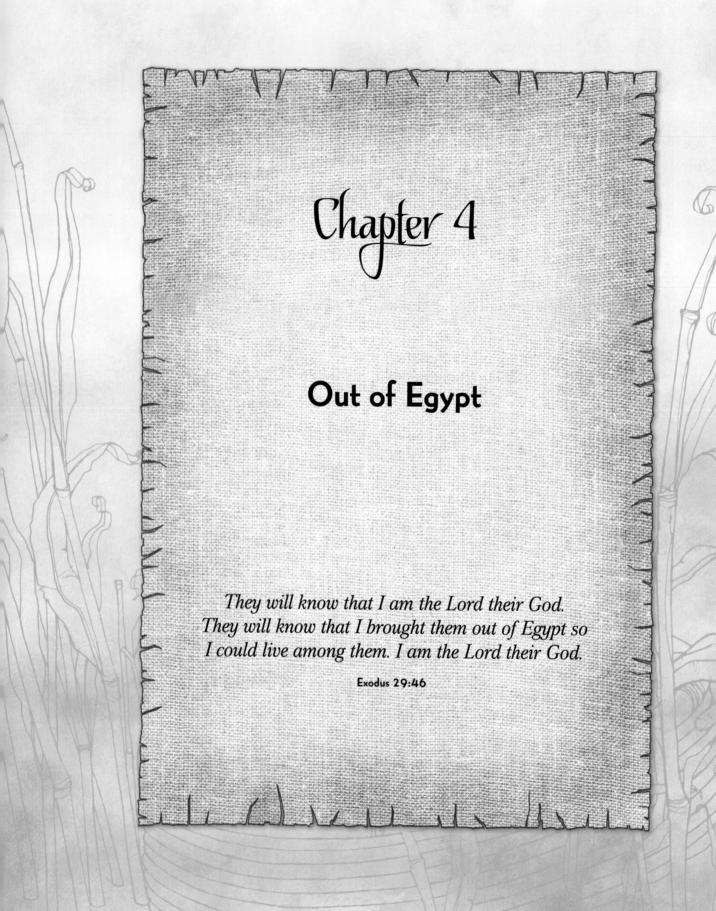

Chapter 4

Out of Egypt

They will know that I am the Lord their God.
They will know that I brought them out of Egypt so
I could live among them. I am the Lord their God.

Exodus 29:46

When Jacob moved his family from Canaan to live with Joseph in Egypt, they were a clan of 70 people. For hundreds of years, God's people lived peacefully and safely in Egypt, and their numbers grew. But then a new Pharaoh took over. He was afraid of God's people because their commitment to God was strong, and they had become a powerful nation just as God had promised. So the king of Egypt forced them to work as his slaves. But God had a plan. He wasn't going to allow his people to be slaves forever. God would lead them to the land he had promised. But first God had to find a leader to guide his people into freedom.

Moses Becomes a Leader

Exodus 1–4

A Hebrew woman named Jochebed gave birth to a beautiful baby boy. Pharaoh wanted all the Hebrew baby boys killed, so Jochebed hid her precious child to keep him safe. "Please, God, help save my son," she prayed. Jochebed placed the baby in a basket and floated it in the Nile River. Miriam, the baby's sister, watched from a distance.

When Pharaoh's daughter came to the river to bathe, she spotted the basket in the reeds. "Poor child," said the princess. "He is a Hebrew baby. I will keep him as my own and call him Moses, because I brought him out of the water."

Moses became the son of the princess. He grew up in the palace in Egypt. But when Pharaoh tried to kill him for harming an Egyptian, Moses ran away to the desert.

Moses lived in the desert of Midian for many years. One day on Mount Horeb, the mountain of God, Moses noticed a bush covered in flames. He wondered, *Why isn't the bush burning up?*

Suddenly a voice boomed out of the flames. "Moses! Moses! Do not come any closer. I am the God of Abraham, Isaac, and Jacob. I have heard the cries of my people. I am going to rescue them. Go back to Egypt. Tell Pharaoh to let my people go!"

Moses was shaking. "No, Lord, not me. Who am I to talk to Pharaoh? Send somebody else."

"I will be with you, Moses. Here is a sign to show that I sent you. Throw your staff on the ground, and it will turn into a snake."

Moses did as God instructed, and a snake slithered on the ground where the staff had been. Moses grabbed the snake's tail, and it turned into a staff again. Moses saw God's power. Now Moses was ready to lead God's people.

God's Message

I have heard the cries
of my people,
longing to be free.

I will come to their aid;
I will break the bonds
that tie them.

I will show the people
of Egypt that there is
no God greater than me.

Signs and Wonders

Exodus 7:14—14:31

Moses entered Pharaoh's throne room. "The God of the Hebrews wants his people to worship him in the desert. Let the people go and worship God."

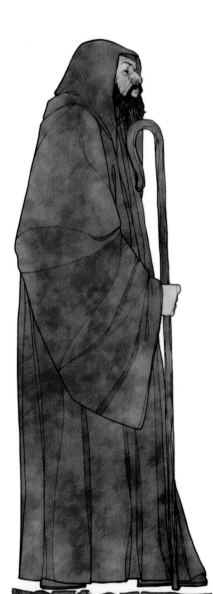

"No," Pharaoh said. "I need them here."

"God Almighty is angry with you, Pharaoh. He will cause things to happen if you don't listen."

So God sent a plague. The Nile River flowed red with blood. The water in all the ponds, pools, and fountains turned to blood.

"Make it stop!" cried Pharaoh. So Moses prayed to God, and the water in Egypt flowed clean and sweet and clear again.

A week later, Moses went to Pharaoh. "Let my people go."

Pharaoh said, "No."

So God sent a second plague to show Pharaoh his power. Frogs invaded Egypt. They splashed in the water. They rolled in the dirt. They climbed in the windows and jumped on the beds.

"Make it stop!" cried Pharaoh. So Moses prayed to God, and the frogs jumped back into the Nile River where they belonged.

Then God sent a third plague, and dust on the ground turned into tiny, nasty gnats. They buzzed in the air. They landed on the people and the animals.

Moses went to Pharaoh again and said, "Let my people go."

Pharaoh said, "No."

So God sent a fourth plague. Thick swarms of flies poured into Pharaoh's palace and the houses of the Egyptians. Every building, every barn, every porch and kitchen was covered with flies.

"Make it stop!" cried Pharaoh. So Moses prayed to God, and all the flies flew away.

Then God sent a fifth plague. All the livestock in the fields of Egypt died. The horses and donkeys, camels and cattle, sheep and goats fell over dead.

But Pharaoh would not let God's people go.

Then God told Moses to throw handfuls of soot from the furnace into the air. He did, and nasty sores called boils broke out on the people and the animals. That was the sixth plague.

Moses went to Pharaoh and said, "Let my people go."

Pharaoh said, "No."

So God sent a seventh plague. He sent hail and thunder and lightning. It was the worst storm Egypt had ever seen. The hail flattened the crops in the field and stripped the leaves off the trees.

"Make it stop!" cried Pharaoh. So Moses prayed to God, and the hailstorm ended.

Then God sent the eighth plague. Swarms of locusts covered the land. They ate all the plants and every tree. The insects filled the houses of Pharaoh and all the Egyptians.

"Make it stop!" cried Pharaoh. So Moses prayed to God, and the wind blew the locusts away.

Then God told Moses to point to the sky. Moses did, and suddenly a thick darkness covered Egypt. For three days the people couldn't see anything. That was the ninth plague.

God told Moses he had one more plague. "At midnight," the Lord said, "I will go through the land of Egypt. Every first-born son in every household will die. But my people will be safe. This will be the worst plague of all. Then Pharaoh will let my people go." It all happened just as God said.

"Get out, NOW!" cried Pharaoh. "Take what you need and leave!"

So Moses led God's people out of Egypt.

Moses led the people through the desert to the shore of the Red Sea. The people looked straight ahead and saw only water. They turned around and saw Pharaoh's army charging across the desert.

"We are going to die!" they cried.

"Don't be afraid! The Lord will fight for you!" Moses said. "Be calm and watch what God will do."

Moses raised his staff toward the sea. Suddenly the wind blew and the water piled up into huge walls, leaving a dry path through the center of the Red Sea. The people walked to the other side on the dry ground God provided.

Pharaoh's chariots and soldiers raced after the people. When the entire army was in the middle of the sea, God made the walls of water crash in on them. The sea swallowed the Egyptian army, the chariots, and the horses. But God's people were safe on the other side.

God's Message

I am your heavenly Father,
watching over you
night and day.

I will love you
and protect you
wherever you go.
I will save you
even when you think
things are impossible.

By my power
I will show the nations
that you are my people
and I am your God.

Chapter 5

New Rules for Holy Living

Moses went and told the people all of the Lord's words and laws. They answered with one voice. They said, "We will do everything the Lord has told us to do."

Exodus 24:3

The miraculous opening and closing of the Red Sea was only the beginning of God's powerful way of providing for his people. As the nation of over two million people made their way through the desert of Sinai, they quickly finished the bread and water they had taken from Egypt. When they were thirsty, God provided water. When they needed food, God sent bread from heaven each morning and quail in the evening. When God's people were attacked, he gave them victory in battle. God promised to be with his people … and he was. He did far more for them than they could ever imagine.

Straight from the Mountaintop

Exodus 20

The great mountain rumbled and boomed like an earthquake.

The smoky skies clapped with a thousand thunderbolts.

"HELP!" the people cried out as they ran for cover.

"SETTLE DOWN! SETTLE DOWN!" shouted Moses.

The people gathered below the mountain, ready to listen to their leader. Moses stood high above all the people so they could hear his voice.

"I've been on the mountain with God for forty days and forty nights. He gave me special rules for us to live as his holy people."

Moses held up two stone tablets and read the rules to the people.

God is number one.
There is no other god
except our God.

Praise God every day
and only worship him.
There is nothing else worth worshiping.

Always use respectful words
when you speak about God.

Have one special day a week
to rest and praise God.

Honor your father and mother.
Obey them, answer when they call, be kind
to them, and always show love toward them.

God's Message

Be kind to everyone.
It is wrong to hurt another person,
because everyone is special to God.

Husbands and wives must be loyal to each
other, showing love and kindness always.

Do not steal.
Respect the belongings of others.

Always tell the truth. Sometimes it's hard,
but it's always the right thing to do.

Be happy with what you have. Do not
wish for things that belong to other people.
Everything you have is a blessing from God.

From this day forward,
let my grace guide your
words and your actions.

You are my people,
my chosen ones.

I have set you apart from
all the nations of the world.

Be a shining example
wherever you go.

Chapter 6

Wandering

If the Lord is pleased with us,
he'll lead us into that land.
It's a land that has plenty of milk and honey.

Numbers 14:8

God's rules and laws were perfect, but God's people were not. They wanted to obey the laws, they wanted to live holy lives, but still they made bad choices and did the wrong things.

When they thought God had left them, they made their own god, a calf made out of gold. God was very angry, but when the people said they were sorry, God forgave them.

The Israelites prepared a special tent for God called a tabernacle. God placed a cloud over the tabernacle during the day; at night he appeared as fire. Day or night, the people could see a sign of God's presence as he led them through the wilderness. God provided for his people as they made their way to the land of Canaan.

God's Brave Explorers

Numbers 13

After traveling in the wilderness, Moses and the Israelites reached the edge of Canaan, the land God had promised his people. The weary travelers were excited to know their journey was almost over.

Moses called the people together. "Before we enter this Promised Land, we must send explorers to learn about the land and the people who live there," he said.

Moses chose twelve explorers and gave them instructions. "Go south and then to the mountains," he said. "See what the land looks like. Is the soil rich for planting? Are there lots of trees? Are the people strong or weak? What are the towns like? Are they open like camps, or do they have walls?"

The twelve explorers packed up. Off they went. They searched and looked and investigated for forty days.

Then they returned to Moses with a report. "The land is awesome!" said the explorers. "The soil is good for planting. Just taste these wonderful fruits we found: grapes, pomegranates, and figs." They shared their treasures with the people.

The Israelites couldn't wait to enter the land. Excitement grew among the people.

But when Moses asked about the Canaanites who lived in the new land, the explorers began to disagree. Ten were fearful and told the others, "We can't go there. The cities are huge and they have tall walls around them! The people are big and strong! Some are as big as giants!"

"They will kill us if we try to take their land!" they cried.

The fears of the ten explorers quickly spread through the camp. "We were better off back in Egypt living as slaves," the people protested.

But two explorers, Caleb and Joshua, were not afraid. They were strong and brave, and they trusted God. "We can do it! We can take the land! The Lord is on our side. Don't be afraid of the people. They have no protection, but the Lord is with us."

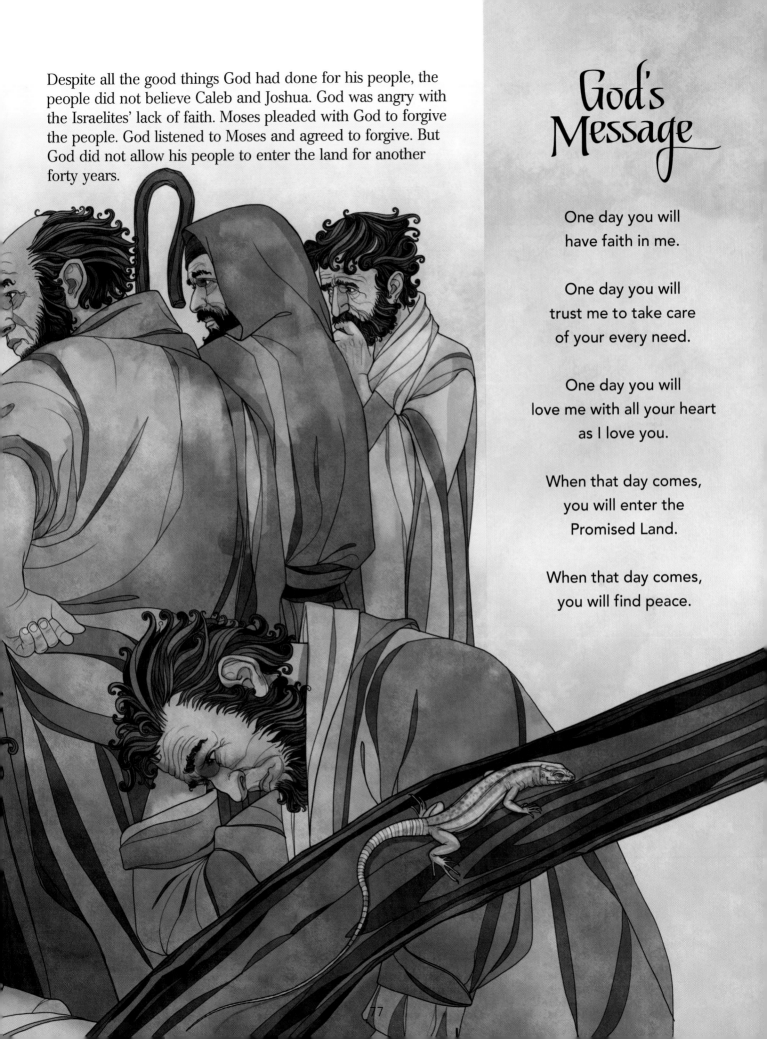

Despite all the good things God had done for his people, the people did not believe Caleb and Joshua. God was angry with the Israelites' lack of faith. Moses pleaded with God to forgive the people. God listened to Moses and agreed to forgive. But God did not allow his people to enter the land for another forty years.

God's Message

One day you will
have faith in me.

One day you will
trust me to take care
of your every need.

One day you will
love me with all your heart
as I love you.

When that day comes,
you will enter the
Promised Land.

When that day comes,
you will find peace.

A Good Man Makes a Mistake

Numbers 20:1–13

Moses tried to be a good leader. He carefully followed God's instructions. He helped the people remember all of God's rules. When the Israelites grumbled, he tried to be patient, but Moses didn't always succeed.

The Israelites could not find water in the desert. Once again, the people forgot how God had provided for them throughout their journey. They fussed and complained. They blamed Moses. "We'll die in this desert if you don't find us water! We should have stayed in Egypt!"

Moses listened. Then as always—he went to God. He asked God to provide water for the people.

God answered his prayer. "Gather the people around," God instructed. "Take your walking stick and go to a rock I will show you. Talk to the rock, and water will flow."

Moses and his brother Aaron gathered the people who were still griping and grumbling. Moses became angry and lost his temper. He shouted at the people for not trusting God. Then Moses smacked the rock twice with his stick. Immediately water gushed out of the rock, enough for all the people and animals.

The people received what they needed, but Moses was punished for his action. Moses had disobeyed God and hadn't given him credit for the miracle. God said, "Because you did not believe me, and because you did not honor me as holy before the people, you will not lead them into the land I will give them."

Moses remained the leader of the people of Israel, but because of his mistake, his leadership ended at the edge of the Promised Land.

God's Message

I have cared for you
since the day
you left Egypt.

I have provided
your food and
quenched your thirst.

I have protected you
from all threat of danger.

But still I yearn
for your trust
and your love.

How long must I wait?

Chapter 7

The Battle Begins

*"Be strong and brave. Do not be terrified.
Do not lose hope. I am the Lord your God.
I will be with you everywhere you go."*

Joshua 1:9

For the next forty years, God's people
wandered around in the wilderness. They needed
this time to learn to trust God for everything
and to become a strong and mighty nation.

The great leader Moses grew very old and brought
the people to the edge of the Promised Land
once again. When Moses died, Joshua became
the new leader of the Israelites.

God chose Joshua for this job and gave him
great encouragement. "Remember, I am with
you wherever you go," said the Lord.

Taking control of the Promised Land was
not going to be easy. There were many cities
and armies to conquer. But God's people
were ready. They had the strongest weapon
on their side—the Almighty God.

A Win for God's People

Joshua 5:13—6:27

Joshua began to think about the battle to come. Jericho, large and sturdy, would be a challenge for most armies. But Joshua wasn't worried. *The Lord is on our side*, he reminded himself. Even God's unusual plan for victory didn't concern the leader. He had witnessed God's power all his life and trusted that God's plan would work.

God told Joshua that it would take seven days to conquer Jericho. On the first six days, the army marched around the city once each day. Seven priests blowing trumpets made of sheep's horns marched along with them.

On the seventh day, the army got ready at dawn and began their daily maneuvers around Jericho. They marched seven times around the walls of the city. Then God's big plan came into action. The seventh time around, Joshua commanded: "The Lord has given us this city! Now shout, soldiers, shout!"

The priests blew their trumpets as hard as they could. The soldiers shouted with all their might. The walls of Jericho shook and came crashing down.

Joshua and his army walked right into Jericho and claimed it for the Israelite people, just as God had promised.

God's Message

Here is the land
I promised so long ago.

Rejoice in your victory!

And let my name be known
among the nations that
I am the one true God,
and you are
my chosen people.

Chapter 8

A Few Good Men and Women

In those days Israel didn't have a king.
The people did anything they thought was right.

Judges 21:25

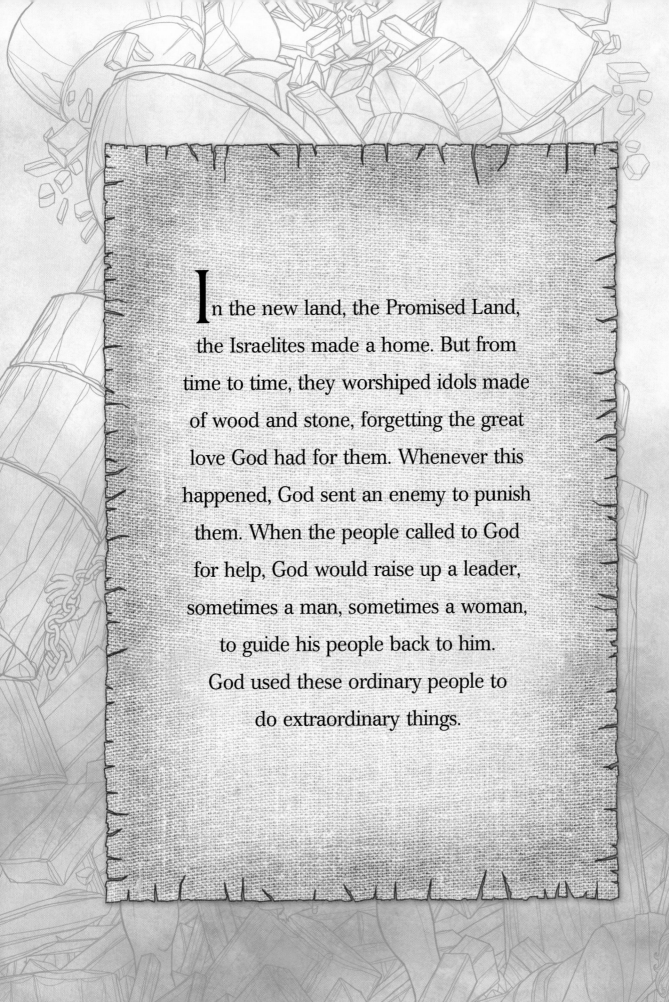

In the new land, the Promised Land, the Israelites made a home. But from time to time, they worshiped idols made of wood and stone, forgetting the great love God had for them. Whenever this happened, God sent an enemy to punish them. When the people called to God for help, God would raise up a leader, sometimes a man, sometimes a woman, to guide his people back to him. God used these ordinary people to do extraordinary things.

Just One More Time, Lord

Judges 16

Once again the people lost their way and worshiped idols, forgetting what God had done for them. So God allowed the Philistines to control the Israelites.

Then the people cried out to God to forgive them and save them from their enemy.

God answered their cries for help and sent a powerful man named Samson to help them fight the Philistines. Samson had a special gift from God. He was blessed with great strength. Once he fought a roaring lion with his bare hands. And he won!

Samson killed many Philistines all by himself. "We have to find a way to get rid of him," the Philistines plotted.

Samson was madly in love with Delilah. Delilah only pretended to love Samson because the Philistines promised her money if she discovered what made Samson so strong.

Delilah tried to trick Samson into telling the secret of his strength. Samson knew he should not tell his secret to anyone, so he tried to trick Delilah too. First he told her that being tied with new leather straps would weaken him enough to be captured.

The Philistines tried it. It didn't work. Samson broke the leather straps as if they were made of air.

Delilah tried again. "If you really love me, you will tell me your secret," she said. Samson made up another story. "I'll lose my power if someone ties me with new ropes."

While Samson slept, Delilah tied him up. Again, the Philistines tried to capture him, but Samson snapped the ropes like tiny threads.

Delilah really wanted that money, so she said, "You lied! If you love me, tell me your secret."

Samson could not stand her nagging anymore. He finally gave in and told Delilah the secret of his strength. "It's my hair. It's never been cut. If someone shaved my head, I would lose my strength and be as weak as any other man."

Delilah waited for Samson to fall asleep. Then she cut his hair. When the Philistines came, Samson couldn't fight them off. The Philistines treated him badly, blinding him and putting him in jail.

One day, the Philistine rulers brought Samson to the temple to show off their prize prisoner. They chained him to two temple pillars. They bragged and made fun of the once-powerful Israelite. Samson prayed and asked God to give him strength just one more time so he could defeat the Philistines. God listened and answered Samson's prayer.

Then Samson pushed on the pillars with all his might, and the temple came crashing down. All the Philistines were killed. Samson died too, but he was remembered as a man of great power who knew his strength came from the Lord.

God's Message

I am God Almighty.

My strength shines
through the leaders
of my people.

Call on me
and I will answer.

I will use my power
to raise you up.

Chapter 9

The Faith of a Foreign Woman

*But Ruth replied, "Don't try to make me
leave you and go back. Where you go I'll go.
Where you stay I'll stay. Your people will be my people.
Your God will be my God."*

Ruth 1:16

Over time, a great famine came to the land of Israel. Naomi, her husband, and their two sons moved to the land of Moab. There the boys grew up and married two women from that foreign land. Everyone was happy. But years passed and Naomi's husband and sons died. Now the women were alone. Naomi told her sons' wives she was going to return to Bethlehem.

Sadness Turned to Joy

Ruth 1-4

Ruth ran down the road after Naomi. "Wait!" Ruth called. "Wait for me!"

Naomi stopped and turned to see her daughter-in-law racing to catch up with her. The older woman put down her belongings and shook her head. "No, Ruth. You must stay here. Moab is your home; your parents live here. It would be best for you to be with them."

"But I will be sad if you leave without me. Wherever you go, I will go too."

There on the road, Ruth made her choice. She and Naomi had been through so much together. It was time to start a new life.

"You are truly a daughter to me," said Naomi. "We will go together."

When the two women arrived in Bethlehem, all the townspeople welcomed them. They remembered Naomi. They were happy to have her back in their neighborhood. When they learned about Ruth's kindness to Naomi, the people were pleased to be her friend too.

Ruth and Naomi made a home in Bethlehem. Even though they were very poor, they thanked God for providing for them.

Each day, Ruth tried to find food for herself and Naomi. Her mother-in-law suggested she go into the fields owned by a rich man named Boaz. "He is my relative, so he will take care of us."

Every day, Ruth went to the fields of Boaz. As the harvesters finished cutting the stalks of grain, Ruth followed them to gather what was left behind.

One day, Boaz noticed Ruth. Boaz was a generous man. He told his workers to let Ruth gather as much grain as she wanted. He shared his lunch with her and sent home extra food for Naomi. Soon Boaz and Ruth fell in love.

Naomi was grateful to God that Ruth had found a good man to marry. After a while, Ruth and Boaz had a baby boy named Obed.

Ruth and Naomi's sadness had turned to joy.

God's Message

I have chosen you
for a journey.
Trust in my plan.

You will have a son
whose son will father
the great king David.

This line of kings will
rule Israel for
hundreds of years.

From them,
the King of Kings
will come and rule forever.

Chapter 10

Messages from God

I prayed for this child.
The Lord has given me what I asked him for.

1 Samuel 1:27

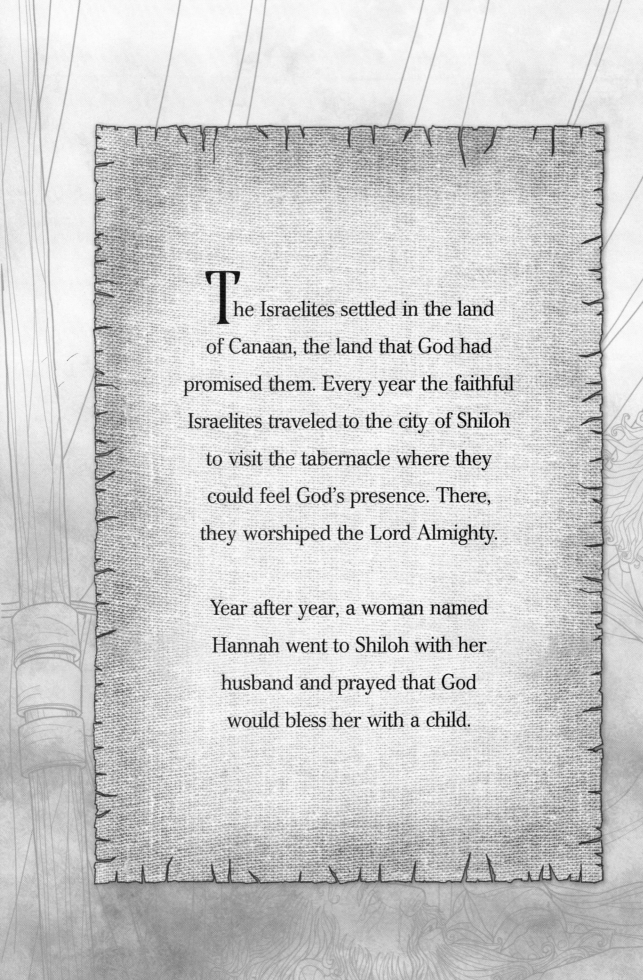

The Israelites settled in the land of Canaan, the land that God had promised them. Every year the faithful Israelites traveled to the city of Shiloh to visit the tabernacle where they could feel God's presence. There, they worshiped the Lord Almighty.

Year after year, a woman named Hannah went to Shiloh with her husband and prayed that God would bless her with a child.

The Listeners

1 Samuel 1, 3

One day, when Hannah was praying in the tabernacle, a priest named Eli saw her. She prayed so hard that tears rolled down her cheeks.

Someday, dear heavenly Father, please give me a child of my own.

God listened to Hannah's request for a child. He felt compassion for her and answered her prayer. He sent her a son named Samuel. Hannah's heart was full of joy. She was grateful that God listened to her prayers.

When Samuel was no longer a baby, Hannah took him to Eli at the tabernacle. "Do you remember me?" she asked Eli. "I prayed for this child," said the mother, "and God answered my prayer. I promised God that Samuel would serve him all his life. So I have brought him to you."

Eli knelt down and took the boy's hand. "I will teach him all I know about God so he will live for God all his days."

Hannah left her son in the care of the priest. Each year she visited Samuel and brought him a new handmade coat. Samuel lived in the temple with Eli. He learned his lessons well and came to love God with all his heart.

One night while sleeping, Samuel heard a voice calling his name. The boy thought it was Eli, so he got up and went to him.

Eli said, "I did not call you. Go back to bed."

A little while later, Samuel again heard a voice calling his name, "Samuel! Samuel!"

He ran to Eli's bedside. "I did not call you," said the weary priest. "Go back to bed."

A third time, Samuel's name was called. A third time, he went to Eli. Now Eli realized what was happening. "God is calling you, Samuel. If he calls you again, say, 'Speak, Lord. I am ready to listen.'"

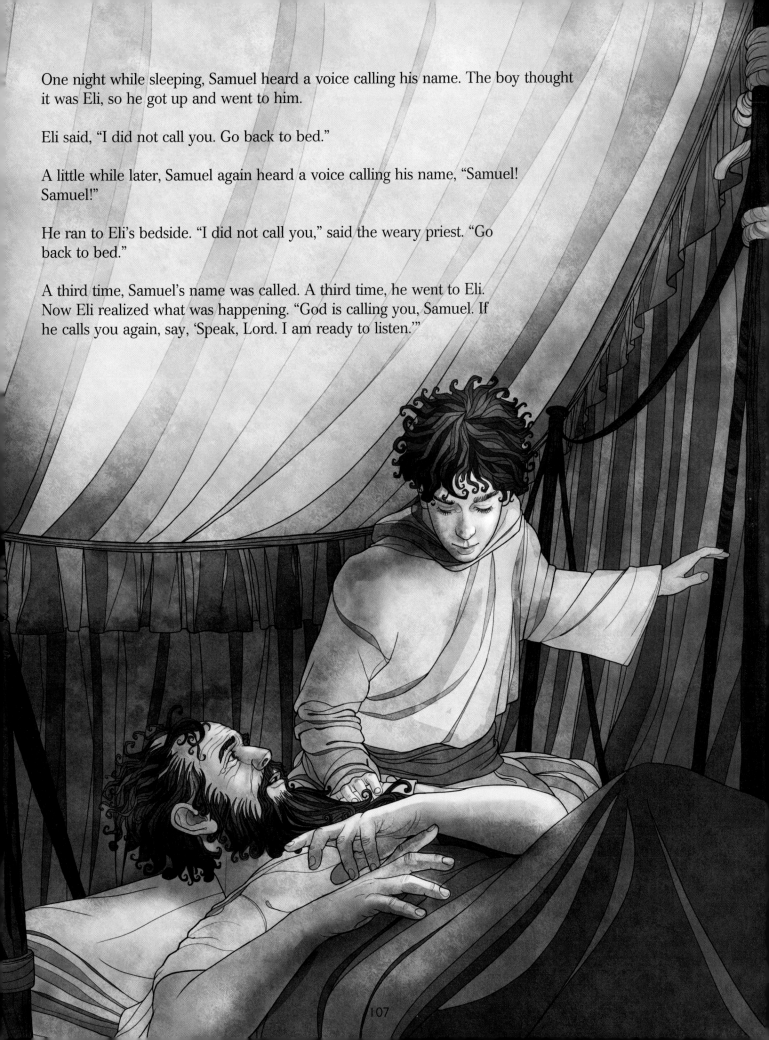

Samuel obeyed. He crawled back into bed and waited and listened.

"Samuel! Samuel!"

This time, the boy didn't go to Eli. Instead he answered the voice. "Speak, Lord. I am your servant. I am ready to listen."

God told Samuel about things that would happen in the days ahead. Samuel listened carefully.

From that night on, God spoke clearly to Samuel. As he grew up, Samuel respected his heavenly Father's words and directions. And the people of Israel knew that Samuel was a good man of God.

God's Message

Be still and listen.
I am calling your name.

My people need a
strong, new leader.

I have chosen you.

You will be a wise
prophet for them.

Through you, they will
hear my words and follow.

Chapter 11

From Shepherd to King

*But the Lord said to Samuel, "Do not consider how
handsome or tall he is. I have not chosen him.
I do not look at the things people look at.
Man looks at how someone appears on the outside.
But I look at what is in the heart."*

1 Samuel 16:7

Samuel grew old and wise and guided the people of Israel. Then the people decided they wanted a king, like the other nations around them. God chose a man named Saul to become king. Saul was a good leader, but he disobeyed God, so God selected a new king—David, the youngest son of a man named Jesse.

No one else saw what God saw. David's father saw his baby boy. David's brothers saw a younger sibling. The townspeople saw an insignificant shepherd. But God saw a king.

Bigger Than a Giant

1 Samuel 17

David was a good-hearted boy who took care of his father's sheep. He was kind to the lambs and loved them. David also loved singing and playing his harp. But more than anything, David loved God.

One day, David's father sent him with bread and cheese to his brothers, who were fighting in King Saul's army. The shepherd boy delivered the food to his brothers and began to talk to the troops. "How is the battle going?" he asked.

"Not so good," answered the soldiers. "Our enemy has a giant named Goliath on their side—look at him over there on that hill. He's going to kill us all!"

David looked at Goliath. *Bigger than big*, thought the boy.

But Goliath's size did not bother David. He marched up to King Saul and volunteered to fight.

"You?" The king laughed. "Is this a joke?"

David spoke up. "I have killed a lion and a bear all by myself! The Lord who rescued me from the lion and bear will save me from Goliath!"

King Saul replied, "Well, all right. Go ahead and try." He gave David armor and a helmet, but they were too big for the boy. "All I need is my sling," David said.

David stopped at a stream to gather five smooth stones. Goliath laughed at the sight of the small boy. But David wasn't afraid. He put a stone in his sling and whirled it at the giant.

The stone clobbered Goliath right in the head.

The enormous Philistine toppled to the ground.

The Israelites cheered for the little warrior. David won the battle!

God's Message

You shall become
a great warrior and
leader of my people.

I have chosen you not for
your riches or your name
or your appearance,
but for the tenderness and
gentle kindness you show
when tending your sheep.

I have been won over
by your heart.

You will serve my people well.

Chapter 12

A Good King
Makes a Bad Choice

God, create a pure heart in me.
Give me a new spirit that is faithful to you.

Psalm 51:10

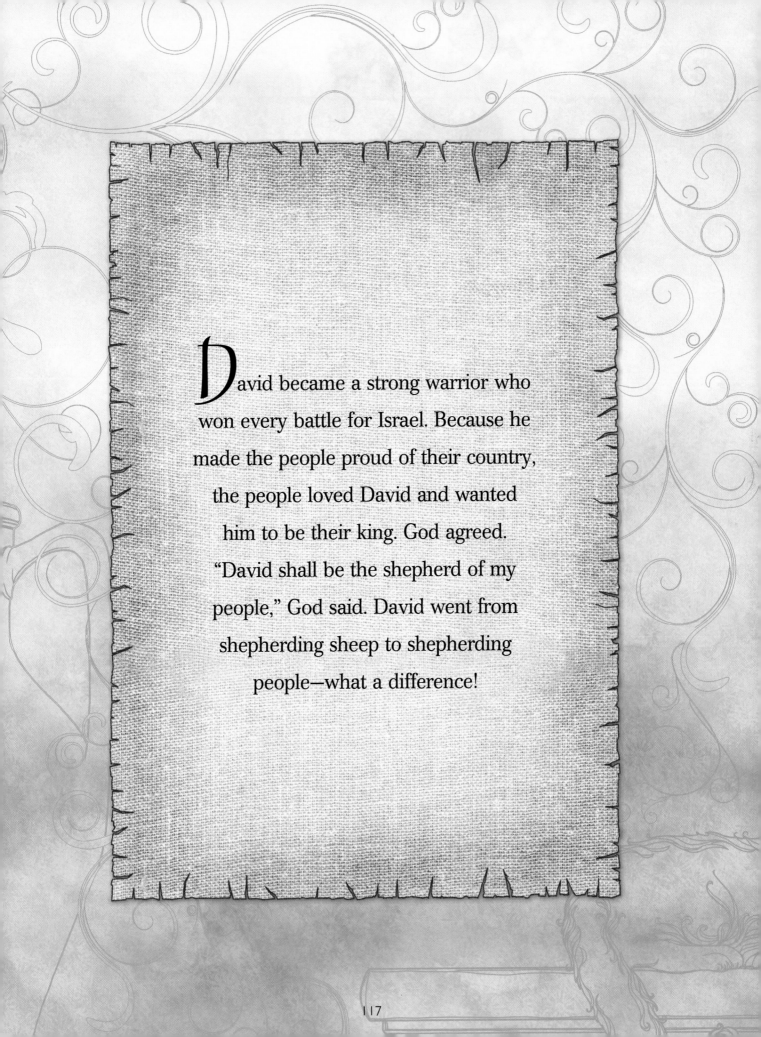

David became a strong warrior who won every battle for Israel. Because he made the people proud of their country, the people loved David and wanted him to be their king. God agreed. "David shall be the shepherd of my people," God said. David went from shepherding sheep to shepherding people—what a difference!

A Selfish Decision

2 Samuel 11–12

King David ruled Israel for many years. He was a good king, and most of the time he made good decisions. But one time King David made a bad choice. He fell in love with another man's wife!

Beautiful Bathsheba was already married to Uriah. But King David loved Bathsheba so much he could hardly think of anything else.

"I'll get rid of Uriah and then Bathsheba can be my wife," David plotted. He made a plan for Uriah to be killed in a battle, so he could be with Bathsheba.

King David got what he wanted. Bathsheba became his wife. King David was happy until his friend Nathan told him that God was not pleased with what he had done. It was wrong to kill Uriah and take his wife.

David's heart ached. It made him sad to know he had disappointed God. This was a time of many hardships in David's life. He was a king. He had riches, a beautiful palace, and a family. But more than all of that, David wanted God's love. He asked God to forgive him.

Later, Nathan told David, "God has forgiven you for the bad choice you made."

David wrote a song about how much God cared for him.

The Lord is my shepherd;
he is everything I need.
God shows me his beautiful creation.
He helps me see the goodness in the world.
God helps me be strong, in all times.
When I'm sad or worried,
my God comforts me.
He shows me how to live a life
that pleases him.
Even in bad times, I can be brave,
because God will never leave me.
God, your strength makes me
strong and calms me down.
You guard me day and night.
You bless me with your love.
I am sure that your goodness
and love will fill my heart, all my life,
and one day I will live
with you in heaven, forever.

God's Message

Your song of
praise rises sweetly
to the heavens.

My heart overflows.

Your desire to do my will
has brought you grace.

This kingdom
will last forever.

Someday I will send
my only Son to earth.

He will be born into
the family of David,
and he will reign as
King of heaven and earth
forever and ever.

Chapter 13

The King Who Had It All

"May the Lord your God be praised.
He must take great delight in you.
He placed you on the throne of Israel.
The Lord will love Israel for all time to come.
That's why he has made you king.
He knows that you will do what is fair and right."

1 Kings 10:9

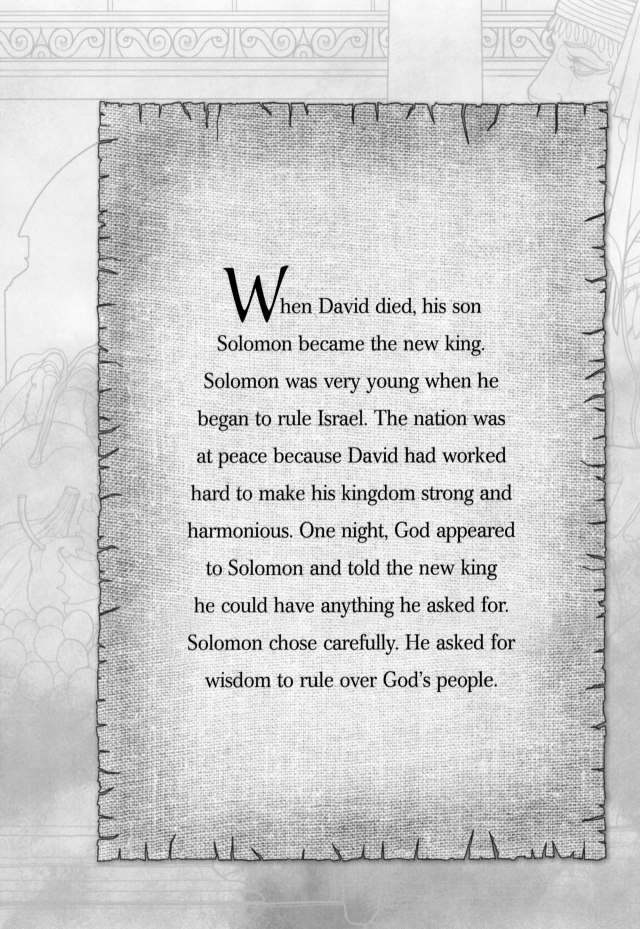

When David died, his son
Solomon became the new king.
Solomon was very young when he
began to rule Israel. The nation was
at peace because David had worked
hard to make his kingdom strong and
harmonious. One night, God appeared
to Solomon and told the new king
he could have anything he asked for.
Solomon chose carefully. He asked for
wisdom to rule over God's people.

A Royal Visitor

1 Kings 10

King Solomon loved God, so he built a temple where God would
dwell and the people would worship him. Solomon planned
it to be the most beautiful building in the country.
Nations all around Israel heard about Solomon.
They knew he was the wisest and richest man
in the world. They knew he had built a great
palace, a beautiful temple, and grand cities.

One day, the Queen of Sheba came to visit King Solomon. A colorful parade of royalty with servants, assistants, and government officers arrived in Jerusalem after traveling more than a thousand miles.

What a sight! The rich and famous queen was carried through the streets in a brilliant caravan. With her came carts full of treasures. Trunks overflowed with gold, precious jewels, and rare, sweet-smelling spices. All were gifts for King Solomon.

The colorful caravan made its way to the palace. The king himself waited on the steps to welcome his guest.

"King Solomon," said the queen, "I've heard about your great wisdom and knowledge. I have also heard about your golden palace and the beautiful temple you built for your God. I have come to see everything for myself and to ask you many questions."

The king showed his guest around the temple and the palace. He answered every one of the queen's questions. No question was too difficult for Solomon. His vast knowledge amazed her. He knew about plants and animals. He understood what made people act the way they do. During her visit, the queen learned a lot from the wise king of Israel. She could see that God favored Solomon and had blessed him greatly.

Soon the visit came to an end, and it was time for the queen to return to her homeland. Before she left, the Queen of Sheba told King Solomon, "Your wisdom and wealth are much greater than I had heard or imagined. Your people are blessed to have you as their king."

Stories of Solomon and his wisdom were told throughout the nations of the world. Solomon wrote more than one thousand songs, and he wrote down many of his wise thoughts so the people could share the wisdom that God had given him.

God's Message

I have given you wisdom
to surpass the
wisest men on earth.

Great wealth and fame
are yours as well.

Use the gifts I have
given you wisely,
and I will bless you
and my people Israel.

Chapter 14

A Kingdom Torn in Two

So the Lord said to Solomon,
"You have chosen not to keep my covenant.
You have decided not to obey my rules.
I commanded you to do what I told you.
But you did not do it. So you can be absolutely
sure I will tear the kingdom away from you.
I will give it to one of your officials."

I Kings I I:I I

The wisest man on earth wasn't always wise. As King Solomon grew older, he began to make bad choices. He married many women who worshiped idols. Instead of leading them to love God, Solomon let his wives talk him into worshiping their idols.

After Solomon's rule ended, the peace and prosperity of the nation ended too. A dark time began in Israel's history. Men fought over who would be king. The kingdom divided and a long string of evil kings began to rule the nations. Occasionally, a good king would come to the throne and call the people back to God.

Good Kings, Bad Kings

1 Kings 14:21–31; 15:9–24, 29–33

God was very disappointed with Solomon. "Since you have disobeyed me and worshiped other gods, I will tear the kingdom away from you," God told the king.

God was angry with Solomon. The people of Israel were angry too. For years, Solomon had demanded huge taxes from them. This made the people poor, and many of them had turned away from God in discouragement, worshiping false gods instead.

Just as God promised, he split the great kingdom of Israel into two nations, Israel and Judah.

For the next 350 years, God's chosen people did not follow God's rules for holy living. Most of the time they were led by evil kings who worshiped idols instead of the one true God.

One good king of Judah, King Asa, tried hard
to bring the people back to worshiping God.
Asa got rid of the false idols. He brought
gold and silver to the temple to show
honor to God.

Just as Asa tried to do good, King Ahab of Israel seemed determined to do the most evil. He and his wife, Jezebel, encouraged the people to worship the idol Baal. Their actions were more evil than all the other bad kings combined. It was a sad time for the nation that had been led by so many faithful men.

God's Message

You have turned
your backs on me.

Your kings have
led you astray.

The closeness we
once shared is gone.

But I will call you back,
again and again.

I will never stop trying.

I am your loving God
and you are my people.

Chapter 15

God's Messengers

Then I heard the voice of the Lord.
He said, "Who will I send? Who will go for us?"
I said, "Here am I. Send me!"

Isaiah 6:8

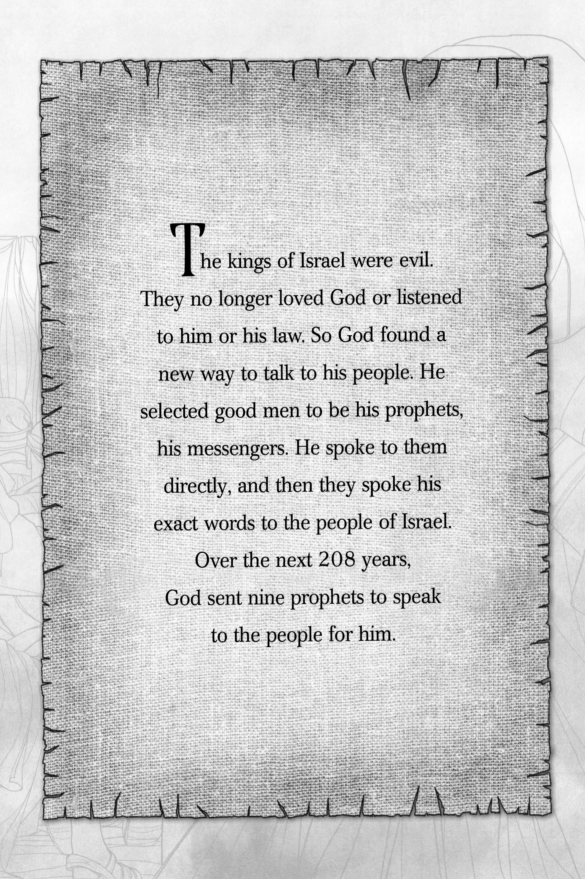

The kings of Israel were evil.
They no longer loved God or listened
to him or his law. So God found a
new way to talk to his people. He
selected good men to be his prophets,
his messengers. He spoke to them
directly, and then they spoke his
exact words to the people of Israel.
Over the next 208 years,
God sent nine prophets to speak
to the people for him.

Courageous Prophet

1 Kings 17–18

A wild-looking man from the desert stormed into the palace and announced to King Ahab: "The one true God of Israel has sent me to tell you that there will be no rain until he decides to send it. Years of drought are ahead."

Elijah was a prophet of God. He was the voice of goodness and the voice of God. Evil King Ahab and his wife, Jezebel, were angry at Elijah; they wanted to kill him. But God kept him safe.

"Go to the Kerith Ravine on the other side of the Jordan River," said God to Elijah. "Stay there and be safe."

Elijah trusted God. He ran to the brook in the ravine and camped there for a long time. Every morning and evening, God sent ravens with bread and meat for Elijah, so he never went hungry. Elijah rested, waiting for God to direct him.

Finally, God told Elijah to speak again to Ahab. When Ahab saw Elijah coming, he said, "So it's you! You are the reason we have had no rain!"

"The drought was your fault, not mine," replied Elijah. "You turned away from God and worshiped the false god Baal."

Elijah challenged Ahab. "If you don't believe me, let's see whose god is the true God."

Ahab eagerly accepted the challenge. He gathered all the people and all the priests of Baal at Mount Carmel. There Elijah explained the test. They would see whose god could start a fire on an altar. The Baal priests prepared an altar and prayed to Baal for fire. Nothing happened. The priests prayed all morning long. No fire. They whooped and hollered, jumping up and down, begging Baal for fire. Nothing happened.

Finally, Elijah took his turn. To make the challenge even harder, he drenched the altar with water.

Elijah prayed, "O God of Abraham, Isaac, and Israel, show these people that you are the one true God."

Immediately, fire from heaven burned up the altar and the people fell on their knees in worship.

"Now God will send rain," Elijah announced. Soon the sky turned black with storm clouds, the wind blew, and rain poured down on the dry and thirsty ground.

God's Message

You are far from me in spirit
and I cannot reach you.

You are blind to my power,
and deaf to my calls.

But you will hear my voice
through my prophets.

And through their miracles
you will see me.

These messengers who
speak my words will bring
you close to me again.

Elisha, Man of Miracles

2 Kings 2, 5

When Elijah's work on earth was over, God took him to heaven in a spectacular, fiery chariot. As his friend Elisha watched, the chariot rose higher and higher, disappearing into the clouds.

Elisha picked up Elijah's cloak. "Now that my friend is gone, it is my job to be God's voice to the people." There was plenty of work for Elisha to do. People were sick and hungry. But God had given Elisha great power, so the prophet was able to do many miracles that helped the people.

One day, a military commander named Naaman came to Elisha for healing. Naaman had a skin disease called leprosy. No medicine could heal him. Elisha told Naaman to wash himself in the Jordan River seven times to be healed.

Naaman thought the idea was crazy. But his friends persuaded him to do as Elisha had instructed. Naaman dipped himself in the river seven times. His skin was just like new! The miracle convinced Naaman that the God Elisha served was the one true God.

God's Message

Elijah's work is over,
and it is you, Elisha,
who will take his place.

You will be a great
prophet for me.

You will be my voice
to the people.

You will perform miracles
in my name.

Chapter 16

The Beginning of the End

The Lord warned Israel and Judah
through all of his prophets and seers.
He said, "Turn from your evil ways.
Keep my commands and rules.
Obey every part of my Law. I commanded
your people who lived long ago to obey it.
And I gave it to you through
my servants the prophets."

2 Kings 17:13

Elijah and Elisha were prophets who spoke for God to the people of Israel. But Israel would not listen to them. God was angry, but he did not give up. He sent more messengers to speak his words to the kings and to the people, reminding them of his love and asking them to turn back to him. He warned Israel what would happen if they refused, but still they would not listen.

Years later, another great prophet, Isaiah, was called by God to be his voice to the people of Judah. Isaiah reminded the people how important it was to follow God and obey his rules. But no one listened to God's messenger. They forgot all that God had done for them. They didn't care about God's blessings.

Good News, Bad News

Isaiah 3, 40

Isaiah tried to get through to the people, but they wouldn't listen.

"I'll try once more," he said to himself.

"Listen, everyone! God has some good news and bad news for you," Isaiah began.

"God is disappointed that you are disobeying his rules. If you change and turn back to God, he will forgive you and protect you from your enemies. But if you don't change your behavior, you will be punished. This land will be taken over by your enemies. There will be constant sadness and suffering."

But the people did not pay much attention.

"That old prophet—don't listen to him!" they said.

Isaiah tried even harder to make them listen.

"Here's the good news," he said. "Your God, the one true God, still loves you, even when you disobey. So, if you change your ways, God will bring you back to your own land. The evil rulers will go away. God will answer your prayers. God's people will no longer be hungry or thirsty. You will have picnics on the hills and happy days with your children. There will be sheep grazing in the pastures. The Lord will comfort Israel again and make her deserts bloom!"

Faithful Isaiah tried his best to convince the people to make good choices. He knew that many of the people weren't listening and would have to experience the bad news first.

God's Message

Do not be troubled.
You have done your best
to persuade my people
to return to me.

Someday, many years
from now, I will send a Savior
for my people.

He will be their true
hope for the future.

Chapter 17

The Kingdom's Fall

"I know the plans I have for you," announces the Lord.
"I want you to enjoy success.
I do not plan to harm you.
I will give you hope for the years to come."

Jeremiah 29:11

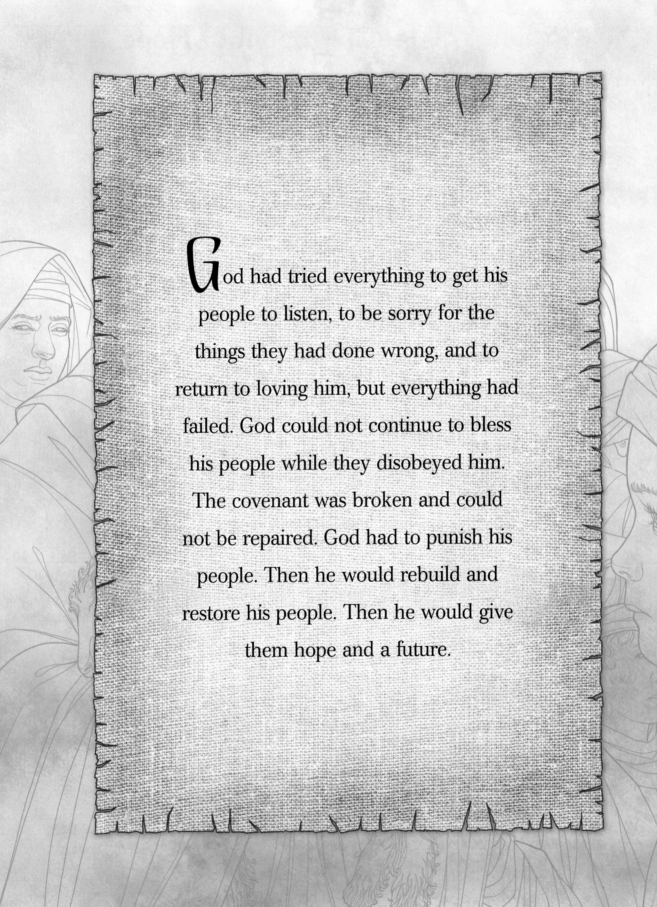

God had tried everything to get his people to listen, to be sorry for the things they had done wrong, and to return to loving him, but everything had failed. God could not continue to bless his people while they disobeyed him. The covenant was broken and could not be repaired. God had to punish his people. Then he would rebuild and restore his people. Then he would give them hope and a future.

Prophet of Tears, Prophet of Hope

Jeremiah 39, 29:1-23

Sparks flew from the burning temple. Citizens ran screaming through the streets. Children wailed for their parents. Soldiers dragged the king and his officers to the outskirts of Jerusalem.

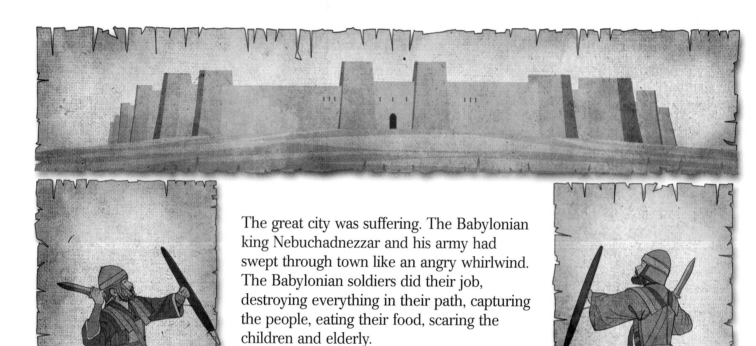

The great city was suffering. The Babylonian king Nebuchadnezzar and his army had swept through town like an angry whirlwind. The Babylonian soldiers did their job, destroying everything in their path, capturing the people, eating their food, scaring the children and elderly.

When the chaos settled down, Jerusalem was ruined, empty, and scorched, the city walls broken down. Smoke rose from the smoldering houses.

And on a nearby hill stood old Jeremiah the prophet, shedding his tears for the city he loved. Crying for the Israelites he tried to save. *Why wouldn't they listen?* he thought. Jeremiah cried, remembering how hard he tried to warn the people. "Turn back to God!" he had told them over and over. But they ignored him and chose to disobey God.

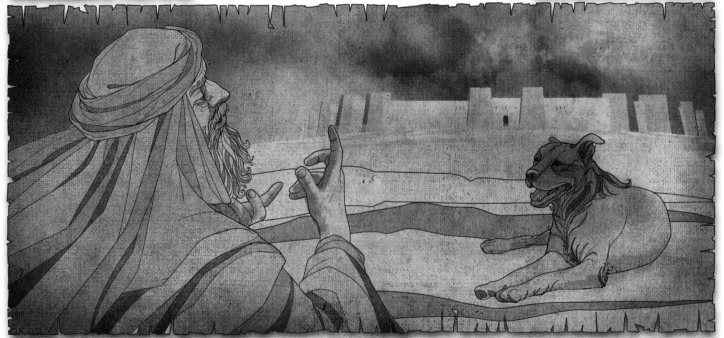

And now the people were being carried off to Babylon to become slaves to the king. King Nebuchadnezzar had spared Jeremiah. The old prophet had one last message for the people. Despite his tears, Jeremiah felt a new hope for the future and he wanted his friends in Jerusalem to believe his words.

"Don't give up hope," the prophet urged. "The Lord is good to those whose hope is in him. If you truly seek him and wait patiently, God will save you."

The sad and suffering people of Jerusalem needed Jeremiah's words. His tears showed them he truly cared. And his words gave them courage in the years ahead, to wait patiently for God to rescue them and return them to their homeland.

God's Message

My love for you
cannot be measured.
It has no beginning
and it never ends.

I will be faithful to you
and love you from
one generation to the next
and far beyond.

Reach out to me, for
I am right here beside you.

Believe in me and have hope.

Chapter 18

God Watches Over Daniel

"I order people in every part of my kingdom to respect and honor Daniel's God. He is the living God. He will live forever. His kingdom will not be destroyed. His rule will never end. He sets people free and saves them. He does miraculous signs and wonders. He does them in the heavens and on the earth. He has saved Daniel from the power of the lions."

Daniel 6:26, 27

The warnings God gave his people about bad things that would happen came true just as God said. The Babylonians captured the best and brightest young people of the nation and took them far away.

Daniel and his three friends were among them. They were chosen to be trained as new leaders of this foreign nation. But instead they chose to follow God's way and his law, even though it was dangerous to disobey the king of Babylon.

Helped by an Angel

Daniel 6

Daniel was one of the captive Jews taken prisoner from Jerusalem. He was very wise and became important in his new home of Babylon. King Darius relied on Daniel to help him make good decisions. The king liked Daniel so much he gave him bigger and better jobs to do. But this made the other officials jealous. They didn't like a captive Jew getting the best jobs and being honored by the king, so they plotted to hurt Daniel.

One day, the officials had a brainstorm. "I've got it!" one of the men said. "Daniel prays to God three times every day. Let's get the king to sign a law making prayer illegal."

The officials quickly convinced the king to sign the law. Now those who prayed to anyone except the king would be thrown into a den of lions!

King Darius was pleased with this new rule; he felt even more powerful and important than ever. But he forgot that his friend Daniel prayed to God.

As soon as Daniel began to pray near his window, the officials ran to the king. "Daniel broke your new law! He's praying to God. Now you'll have to throw him to the lions."

The king was upset. He liked Daniel very much. He told Daniel, "You serve your God so faithfully, maybe he can save you."

Into the lions' den went Daniel.

The king was so worried about his friend, he couldn't sleep. The next morning, King Darius ran to the lions' den and called out. "Daniel? Are you alive?" To his surprise, Daniel answered back.

"My God sent his angel to protect me," said Daniel. "God's angel shut the mouths of the lions. They didn't hurt me at all."

King Darius immediately declared a new law: "In every part of my kingdom, people must worship the God of Daniel. He is the living God—the God who rescues and saves."

God's Message

I am God Almighty.
Great is my power.

I can make the sun stand still.
I can stop fire from burning.
I can close the mouths
of hungry lions.

Great is your trust in me.

Your faith has saved you
and shown the world
I am a loving God who
cares for his people.

Homesick No More

Ezra 3:7—6:22

"Start packing!" King Cyrus announced. "You're going home to Jerusalem! It's time to rebuild the temple, and I'm sending you home to do the job."

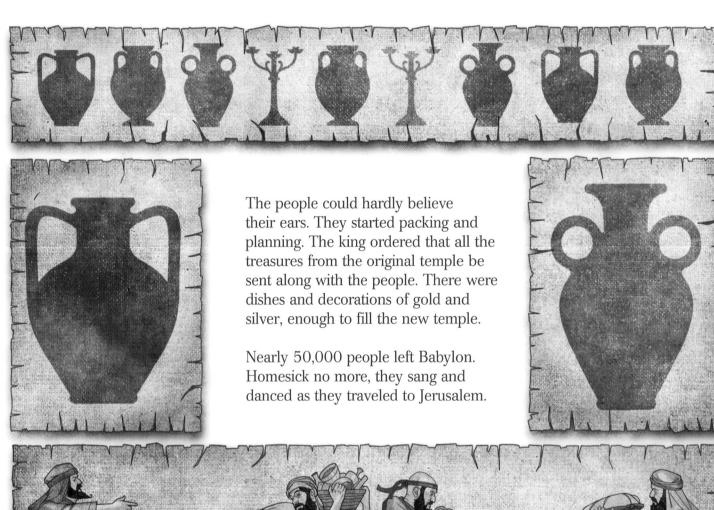

The people could hardly believe their ears. They started packing and planning. The king ordered that all the treasures from the original temple be sent along with the people. There were dishes and decorations of gold and silver, enough to fill the new temple.

Nearly 50,000 people left Babylon. Homesick no more, they sang and danced as they traveled to Jerusalem.

When they arrived, they rebuilt the altar to worship God and thank him for bringing them home. They laid the foundation for the new temple.

Then they celebrated. The people played their instruments and sang praises to God. "The Lord is good; his faithful love continues forever!"

But the local people of Samaria didn't like the Jews coming back to town and building the temple. They fussed and argued and even wrote letters to King Darius. But his answer was, "Leave these people alone and let them build the temple."

Some of the Jews wanted to build their own houses first, so they left the temple work to tend to their own needs. But when God sent messengers to remind them of their assignment, the people went back to working on the temple.

Before long, the beautiful temple was finished. God had brought his people home.

God's Message

Welcome home, my children.
You are back in Jerusalem.

From this day forward
you will be my temple—
not a temple of
stones and rafters,
but a temple of people.

Go now and be my message
that the Creator
of the universe
lives among you.

Chapter 20

The Queen of Beauty and Courage

"What if you don't say anything at this time?
Then help for the Jews will come from another place.
But you and your family will die. Who knows?
It's possible that you became queen
for a time just like this."

Esther 4:14

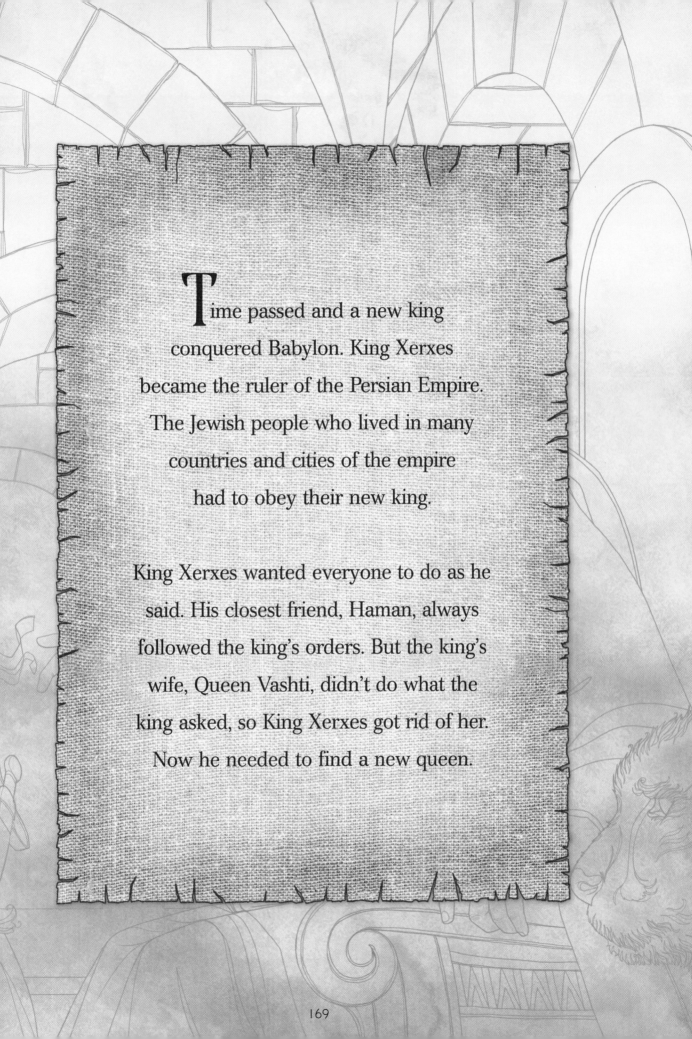

Time passed and a new king
conquered Babylon. King Xerxes
became the ruler of the Persian Empire.
The Jewish people who lived in many
countries and cities of the empire
had to obey their new king.

King Xerxes wanted everyone to do as he
said. His closest friend, Haman, always
followed the king's orders. But the king's
wife, Queen Vashti, didn't do what the
king asked, so King Xerxes got rid of her.
Now he needed to find a new queen.

Esther Saves Her People

Esther 2–8

The search was on for a new queen for King Xerxes of Persia. All the pretty young women were ordered to come to his palace.

Esther didn't want to go, but she had no choice. Her cousin Mordecai warned her: "Don't tell anyone you're a Jew. You might be harmed if they find out!"

Beautiful Esther obeyed. When she was presented to the king, he fell madly in love. King Xerxes quickly made Esther his queen.

But Haman, the king's right-hand man, was growing more powerful. He convinced the king to sign a law that made all the people bow down to Haman. Oh, how Haman loved that rule! Everywhere he went, people knelt down to honor him.

But one day, Mordecai did not bow down to Haman. Mordecai believed it was wrong to show honor to anyone but God. This made Haman very angry. He knew that Mordecai was a Jew, so he convinced King Xerxes to kill all the Jews.

When Mordecai learned of the plan, he ran to Esther. "You must talk the king into changing his plan." Esther wasn't sure she could find the courage to argue against powerful Haman. And what would the king do when he learned she was a Jew? Would she be in danger?

Then Mordecai spoke from his heart. "God may have planned your life just for this moment. You are the only hope for your people."

Esther knew what she had to do. She invited the king and Haman to a special banquet. King Xerxes was so pleased he asked her, "What do you want, Esther? I'll do anything you ask."

Esther said, "I want you to save my life."

The king didn't understand but said, "Of course, I will save your life."

Then Esther explained Haman's plot to kill the nation of Jews.

Angry at Haman's sly trick, the king ordered him killed.

The queen had found her courage. And God's people were saved!

God's Message

Great is your courage.
You have rescued
my people from harm.

You have valued their
safety over your own.

Another selfless one
will follow.

Born to serve,
his love will know
no bounds,
his protection
will be everlasting.

He will lay down
his life to
save my people.

Chapter 21

Rebuilding the Walls

*I said to them, "You can see the trouble we're in.
Jerusalem has been destroyed.
Fire has burned up its gates. Come on.
Let's rebuild the wall of Jerusalem."*

Nehemiah 2:17

Over time, the people of Judah returned home from their exile in Babylon. The first group to return to Jerusalem was very large—about 50,000 people. They rebuilt the temple. The second group of people returned under the leadership of Ezra the priest. A third group returned with Nehemiah. That group started rebuilding the walls around the city of Jerusalem and God's holy temple. It wasn't an easy task because the local people weren't happy and did everything they could think of to stop the work.

Jerusalem: Restored!

Nehemiah 2–4

Nehemiah was living in Persia serving the king. He was sad when he heard that the beautiful city built by David and Solomon was now just a pile of stones.

Nehemiah prayed to God and decided, "I must do something. I will go and help the people rebuild Jerusalem!"

Once he got permission from the king, Nehemiah journeyed to Jerusalem. He was ready to start rebuilding the walls so the people could be protected from their enemies.

While the city slept, Nehemiah and his men rode their horses around the outside of Jerusalem to inspect the broken walls and come up with a plan to fix them.

The next day, Nehemiah gathered the Jewish leaders and explained the plan. "Each citizen will be responsible for repairing the part of the wall that's in front of his home or shop."

The people worked hard and at first the work went well. But then some of their enemies started to cause trouble. They made fun of Nehemiah and his plan. But Nehemiah told them to mind their own business.

When the walls were halfway finished, the builders became tired and discouraged. They worried the neighboring enemies would hurt them while they worked. Nehemiah knew how to encourage the people. "Don't be afraid," said Nehemiah. "Remember the Lord. He is great and powerful."

To protect the new walls and safeguard the people, Nehemiah posted guards. He instructed the workers to carry a weapon. The builders worked with a spear at their side or a sword on their belt. The walls and the people were safe.

When the walls were completed, the people celebrated. The priests and officials divided the people into two groups. They marched around the walls in opposite directions and met at the temple for a thanksgiving service and a great feast.

God's Message

My temple is established,
and you will
worship in peace.

The walls of the
city are restored.

I have brought you back
to your land, my holy city,
as I promised long ago.

I am your God,
and you are my people.

My children,
now you are home.

Chapter 22

The Birth of a King

You will become pregnant and give birth to a son.
You must name him Jesus.

Luke 1:31

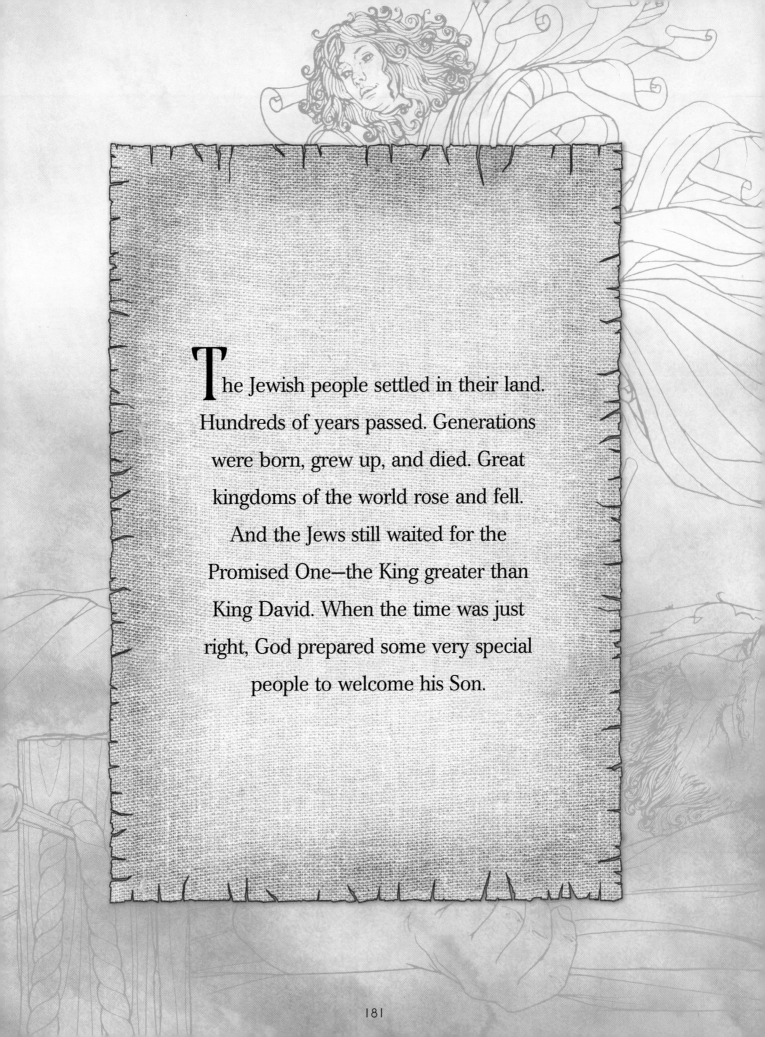

The Jewish people settled in their land. Hundreds of years passed. Generations were born, grew up, and died. Great kingdoms of the world rose and fell. And the Jews still waited for the Promised One—the King greater than King David. When the time was just right, God prepared some very special people to welcome his Son.

Surprised by an Angel

Matthew 1:18-25; Luke 1:26-38

Mary loved her village and the hills around the little town of Nazareth. The morning dew felt cool on Mary's toes as she walked to the well for water.

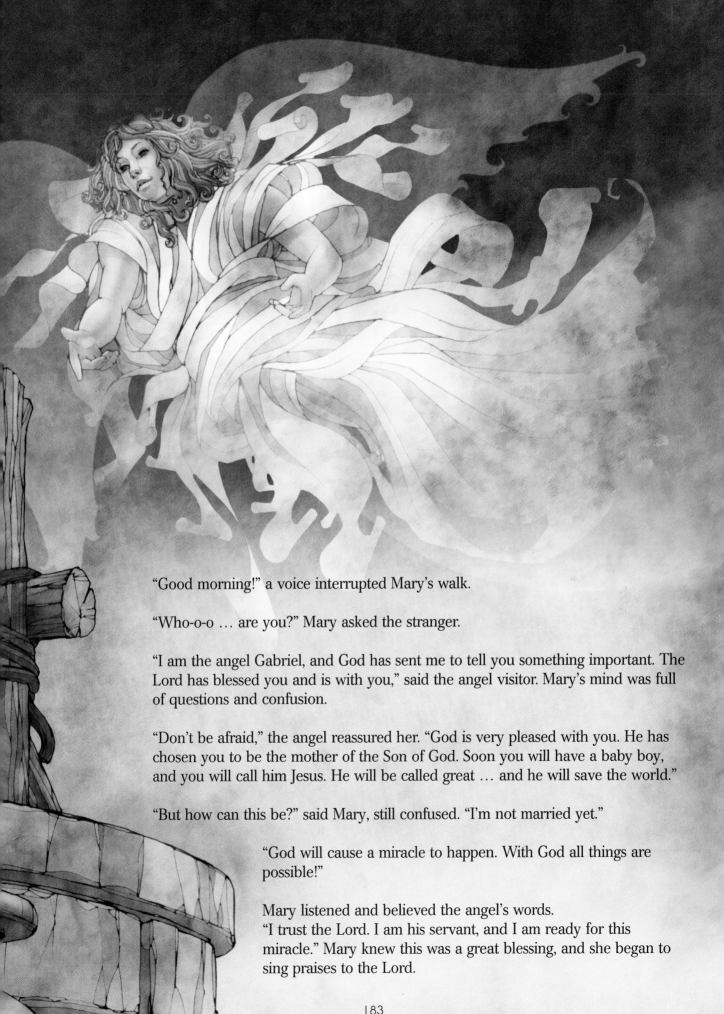

"Good morning!" a voice interrupted Mary's walk.

"Who-o-o … are you?" Mary asked the stranger.

"I am the angel Gabriel, and God has sent me to tell you something important. The Lord has blessed you and is with you," said the angel visitor. Mary's mind was full of questions and confusion.

"Don't be afraid," the angel reassured her. "God is very pleased with you. He has chosen you to be the mother of the Son of God. Soon you will have a baby boy, and you will call him Jesus. He will be called great … and he will save the world."

"But how can this be?" said Mary, still confused. "I'm not married yet."

"God will cause a miracle to happen. With God all things are possible!"

Mary listened and believed the angel's words.
"I trust the Lord. I am his servant, and I am ready for this miracle." Mary knew this was a great blessing, and she began to sing praises to the Lord.

Meanwhile, the angel visited Joseph. He was a good man, and he loved Mary very much. The angel came to Joseph in a dream with the same message. "God has caused a miracle to happen. Even though you aren't married, God's Holy Spirit has caused Mary to be pregnant. She will have a baby boy, and you will name him Jesus. Give him that special name, because it means he will save his people from their sins."

Joseph believed all that the angel said. He was ready to obey. Mary was ready to obey. Together, they waited for the special miracle to come true.

God's Message

I will give the world
a special gift: my Son.

He is the Messiah,
the Prince of Peace—
the one that I
promised to send.

Endless will be his love;
boundless, his power.

He will be the
King of Kings
who saves the world!

Hallelujah!

Luke 2:1–20

Joseph gently lifted Mary onto the donkey's back, and their journey began. "The Roman emperor picked a bad time to make us go to our hometowns!" Joseph complained. "Yes," agreed Mary. "But it's the law. He wants to count his citizens."

The trip to Bethlehem was a hard journey for a woman about to have a baby. Late that night they reached the little town. "I'll find a room so you can rest," Joseph said.

But every inn he tried was full of people. He knocked on door after door and got the same answers: "Full." "No more rooms." "Try down the street."

Mary was very tired. And Joseph was worried. He kept knocking and begging for a room. "Please, we'll take any little corner, anything you have. My wife is about to have a baby!"

The last innkeeper felt sorry for the young couple. "There's a stable in the back. It's small, dark, and with the animals. It's not very clean … "

"We'll take it!"

Joseph made Mary as comfortable as he could in the damp little stable—and not a moment too soon. For that night, her baby boy was born, just as the angel had said. They named the baby Jesus. Mary looked at her beautiful baby, remembering the angel's words. "He will save the world."

That same night, some shepherds were taking care of their sheep in a nearby field. An angel of the Lord appeared to the shepherds, with a glorious light shining all around. The shepherds had never seen such a thing, and they were scared. But the angel calmed them down by saying, "Don't be afraid. I am bringing you good news that will be a joy to all the people. Today your Savior was born in Bethlehem. This is how you will know him—he will be wrapped in cloths and lying in a manger."

Then many angels appeared in
the sky, singing and praising God
for the wonderful gift of baby
Jesus. They sang, "Glory to God
in heaven, and on earth, peace
and goodwill toward men!"

God's Message

The shepherds could hardly wait to meet the baby Savior, so they went straight to town, looking for a baby lying in a manger. When they found Mary, Joseph, and Jesus, they knew that the angel's words were true.

Today my Son has been born as a human.

Like you, he will laugh and cry.

Like you, he will know the love and comfort of family and friends.

Like you, he will experience sadness and pain.

Born to be your Savior, he will live among you and bring you great joy.

He will be your hope and your salvation.

Chapter 23

Jesus' Ministry Begins

Jesus became wiser and stronger. He also became more and more pleasing to God and to people.

Luke 2:52

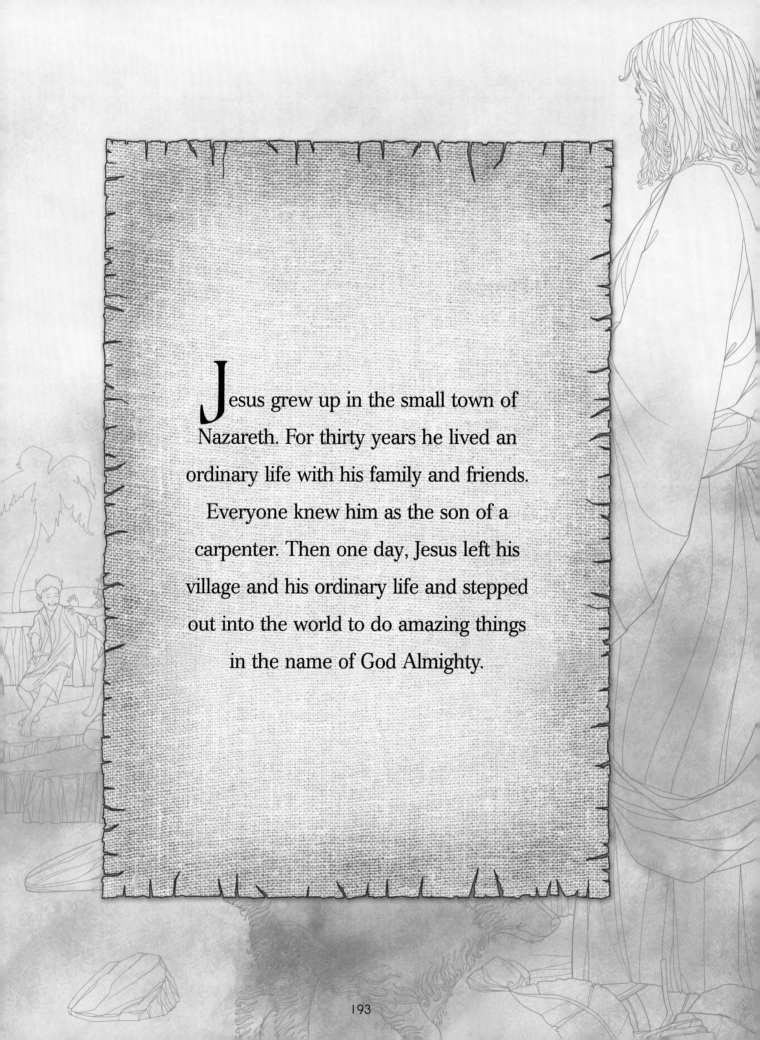

Jesus grew up in the small town of
Nazareth. For thirty years he lived an
ordinary life with his family and friends.
Everyone knew him as the son of a
carpenter. Then one day, Jesus left his
village and his ordinary life and stepped
out into the world to do amazing things
in the name of God Almighty.

A Heavenly Voice

Matthew 3:13–17; Mark 1:9–11; Luke 3:21–22

Just like all the other babies in the world, baby Jesus grew up. He played in the streets of Nazareth with neighborhood boys and girls. He had brothers and sisters and learned how to get along with them. He watched Joseph in his workshop and became a carpenter just like his father. On the outside, he was like all the other Jewish boys in the village. But on the inside, he was very different. He was God's Son.

When Jesus was a grown man, he traveled to the Jordan River where his cousin John was teaching and baptizing people. John's strange appearance and important message were the talk of the countryside. "Be baptized and turn your hearts to God!" John would preach. And many would listen and obey.

The banks of the river were covered with John's listeners when Jesus joined them. Jesus made his way through the crowd. He walked to the shore of the river. He stepped into the deep blue waters of the Jordan and muddied his toes in the soggy riverbed.

Jesus asked John to baptize him. John protested, "No, you should baptize me!" Jesus put his hand on John's shoulder and calmly replied, "It's OK. It is good for us to do this." So there in the Jordan River, John baptized Jesus while all the other men and women watched from the shore.

While Jesus stood in the water, he began to pray. The heavens opened up. The Spirit of God came floating down like a dove and rested on Jesus' shoulder. Then a voice from heaven boomed through the countryside: "This is my Son whom I love. I am very pleased with him."

God spoke. He called Jesus his Son. Now the people knew what God had known all along—this carpenter from Nazareth was very, very special.

God's Message

On this day, the
ordinary ends and
the spectacular begins.

Go tell my people
I have remembered
my promise.

Tell them the
Messiah is here!

The son of a carpenter
in Nazareth is the
Son of God Almighty,
the Creator of the world!

Helping Heart, Healing Hands

Luke 4:38; Luke 5:17–26; Matthew 9:2–8; Mark 2:3–12

Crowds grew quickly when word spread that Jesus was coming. He was becoming well known as a great teacher and healer. Everywhere he went, people gathered to hear his message. And they brought their sick friends and relatives, hoping Jesus would heal them.

In Cana, Jesus made a rich man's son well. At the pools of Bethesda, Jesus healed a man who couldn't walk. In Jerusalem, his touch made a crippled woman well.

In many places, Jesus saw the pain of those who were sick, and he showed his power by healing them.

People who witnessed these miracles saw the power of God, and they believed in Jesus as the Promised Savior. No one else could heal with a touch or a word like Jesus could.

Sometimes the crowds were so large, not everyone could get close enough to hear and see Jesus. Once he preached in a house. It was very crowded. People listened at the doors and windows. A group of men brought their sick friend, hoping Jesus would heal him. But they could not get inside.

The men wouldn't let that stop them. They climbed up on top of the house and cut a big hole in the roof so they could lower their friend down to Jesus.

"Your sins are forgiven," Jesus said to the sick man. "Get up, take your mat, and go home." The man was immediately healed! Everyone who saw the miracle was amazed.

God's Message

You are my Son.
Through your miracles,
my children
see my power.

Through the touch
of your hand,
I heal them.

Through the sound
of your voice,
I comfort them.

Together, we show
our love for all people.

Chapter 24

No Ordinary Man

I and the Father are one.

John 10:30

From the very beginning, the Bible speaks of a King. It was a King who created the world with just a word. It was a King who commanded the water to do remarkable things—to flood the earth, to turn to blood, to divide into two walls so his people could escape. It was a King who sent his people into exile and returned them again to their land. It was a King who was born in Bethlehem.

For centuries the Jewish people were expecting a great king to come and save them. They were thinking the king would be powerful and strong like other world rulers. They were expecting a king with an army to free them from the Romans. But their king, Jesus, was different. He told them, "The time has come. The kingdom of God is near. Repent and believe in the good news." The people were surprised. The high priests were angry. This wasn't the type of king anyone expected.

Hush, Big Wind!

Matthew 8:23–27; Mark 4:36–41; Luke 8:22–25

The people had been following Jesus for days, eager to hear his teaching and hopeful for healings. Jesus hardly had a moment to catch his breath. The crowds were so huge that sometimes Jesus preached to the people on the shore from a boat in the water.

This time, when Jesus climbed into the boat, he simply wanted to rest. He told his disciples, "Let's take the boat to the other side of the sea." As soon as they left the shore, Jesus found a quiet spot in the boat and stretched out for a nap. He slept and slept, while the disciples steered the boat and whispered to each other so they wouldn't disturb him.

Soon the skies turned dark and storm clouds rolled in. The water became choppy; whitecaps slapped the sides of the boat. The gently rocking sea became wildly frightening! Water began to slosh into the boat. The wind howled, thunder boomed, and lightning lit up the sky.

"We're going to drown!" cried the disciples. "Help!" they shouted, holding on to the sides of the boat. But Jesus was still fast asleep! The wind, thunder, and lightning did not disturb him.

"Teacher!" yelled the disciples, trying to wake him up. "Don't you care if we drown?"

Jesus opened his eyes. Then he calmly stood up and spoke to the wind and waves. "Quiet down! Be still!"

The wind and waves obeyed. Immediately, calm returned to the sea. The boat settled back into its gentle rocking rhythm. Jesus turned to the disciples. "Why are you so afraid? Don't you believe in me?"

The disciples, still amazed by what had happened, couldn't even answer. All they could do was wonder, "Who is this man? Even the wind and waves obey him!"

God's Message

You are his disciples,
but you do not understand.

My power is
with him always.

His words melt
hardened hearts.

His gentle touch heals.

His simple commands
control the storm
and the sea.

Someday you will know
that he is my Son.

The Never-Ending Picnic

Matt 14:13–21; Mark 6:32–44; Luke 9:10–17; John 6:5–13

The little boy tugged on Andrew's robe. "Sir?"

Andrew shooed the boy away.

Again the boy tried, "Sir ... Sir ... I can help."

"You? Help? Thanks, but our problem is too big for one little boy," Andrew said, as he tried to keep from laughing at the child's offer.

"I can share my lunch," the boy insisted.

Andrew looked at the thousands of people who had gathered on the hillside to hear Jesus teach. It was getting late, close to suppertime. The crowd would be getting hungry soon. The disciple looked again at the young boy. "Come with me," he instructed. Together, they walked over to Jesus. "This boy would like to share his meal with the people—but it's only five loaves of bread and two fish—not nearly enough for this hungry crowd."

Jesus smiled. "Tell everyone to sit down on the grass," he said.

As everyone settled down, Jesus held up the bread and fish and said a prayer of thanks. He gave the food to the disciples, telling them to share it with all the people. They did as he instructed.

The disciples went through the crowd of thousands, giving food to everyone. The people on that hillside had plenty to eat. There was so much food that twelve baskets full of bread and fish were left over.

The people had come to hear a lesson from Jesus. But instead of hearing a lesson, they saw a miracle! Two little fish and five little loaves were miraculously multiplied by Jesus.

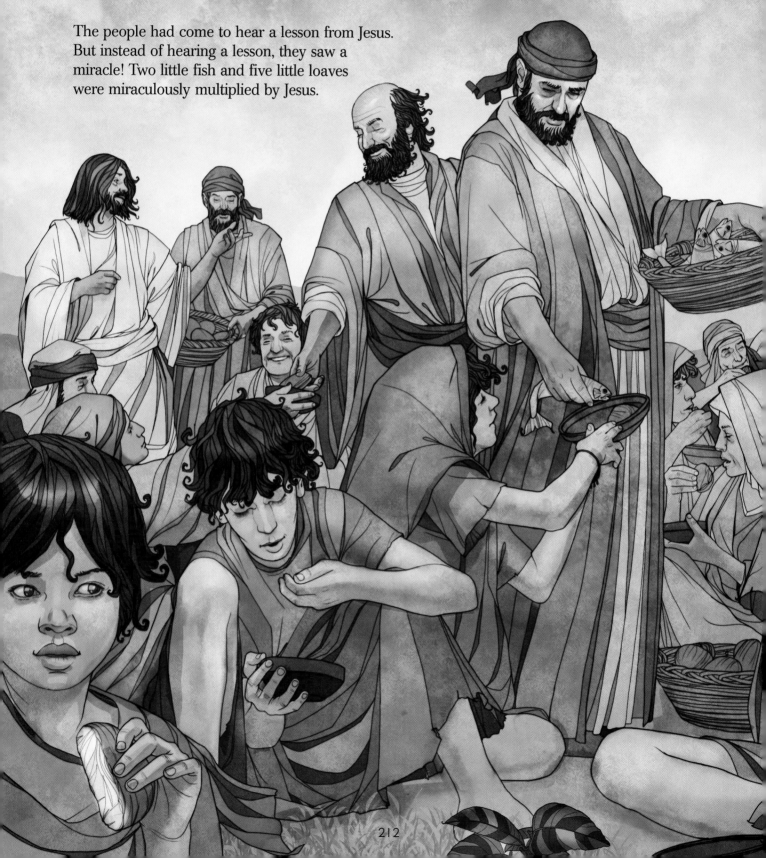

God's Message

You now see that
the smallest child
can bring the largest gift.

Through my power,
a few loaves and fish
can feed a crowd.

Nothing is too small
for me to use
in caring for my people.

Jesus Walks on the Water

Matthew 14:25; Mark 6:48-51; John 6:19-21

Jesus wanted to spend some time alone. While he climbed a hill to find a quiet place to pray, his disciples set sail on the Sea of Galilee to cross over to a town called Capernaum.

During the night the wind stirred up, and Jesus' disciples rowed hard to keep the boat on course. Jesus came down from his praying place and watched the disciples struggling against the wind.

Because he was the Son of God, Jesus could do things that ordinary people could not do. Jesus decided to join his disciples, so he walked out to their boat … on the water!

He walked across the dark water as if it were solid ground. When the disciples saw the shadowy figure moving toward them, they were startled.

Jesus tried to calm them. "Don't be afraid, it's me!" he said.

One of the disciples, Peter, replied, "If it's really you, tell me to come to you on the water."

Jesus said, "Come!" So Peter did. He climbed out of the boat and began walking to Jesus. At first, Peter felt brave knowing that Jesus was near. But when he glanced at the rough waters, his courage disappeared and he began to sink into the sea.

Peter called to Jesus for help, "Lord, save me!" Jesus reached down and pulled Peter up out of the water. Once Jesus and Peter were back inside the boat, the disciples filled the little craft with praise and worship.

The followers now understood who Jesus was, and they said, "Truly, you are the Son of God."

God's Message

Your eyes have
been opened.

At last,
you understand!

Jesus is my Son.

When you look
into his eyes,
I am looking back at you.

The Tears of Jesus

John 11:1-44

One day, as Jesus taught near the Jordan River, a messenger from Bethany rushed over to him. "Lord! Your friend Lazarus is very sick!" said the messenger. "His sisters need you to come right away!" Jesus loved Lazarus and his sisters very much. He visited them often, and they took good care of him.

Jesus pondered the message for a moment and said, "God's Son will be glorified through this illness."

The disciples huddled together, wondering what Jesus meant. Two days later, as they traveled to Bethany, they wondered why Jesus had waited so long to help his friend.

"Our friend has fallen asleep, but I will go and wake him," Jesus said. But the disciples didn't know that Jesus planned to show them a big miracle.

As they neared the village, Lazarus' sister Martha came running to meet them. She told Jesus that Lazarus had died. "Lord, if you had been here, my brother would not have died," she cried. Jesus comforted her. "Your brother will rise again," he said.

Martha thought Jesus meant that Lazarus would live in heaven someday. Jesus asked her if she truly believed in him. "Yes, Lord," she said. "I believe that you are the Son of God."

Then the other sister, Mary, came out to see Jesus. She said, "Lord, if you had been here, my brother would not have died." She cried and cried. Mary cried so hard that Jesus could not keep from crying too.

Jesus, still upset about his friend's death, went to the place where Lazarus' body was buried. The tomb was like a cave with a large rock for a door. "Take the stone away," Jesus ordered. "If you believe, you will see the glory of God."

The disciples didn't understand, but they obeyed. They rolled away the stone. Jesus looked to heaven and prayed, "Father God, thank you for hearing my prayer about Lazarus." Then he turned to the tomb and shouted, "Lazarus! Come out!"

And Lazarus, alive again, came out!

The sisters and all the friends and disciples shouted for joy. They understood that only the Son of God could have done such a miracle.

God's Message

My Son has
seen your tears.

He has heard your cries.

Your sadness has
touched his heart.

He calls to me knowing
I have power over all things,
including death.

Little Children Teach a Big Lesson

Matthew 19:13–15; Mark 10:13–16; Luke 18:15–17

Jesus called to the children playing on the hillside nearby. At the Teacher's calling, the children ran to him. They settled down on the grass beside him, asking questions, telling Jesus their latest adventures.

From a distance, the mothers and fathers watched as Jesus patted their little ones on the head and blessed each child. Jesus loved being with the children. They brought him great joy.

But the disciples considered the children a problem instead of a blessing. They were upset that the children were interrupting Jesus. They thought Jesus should tend to more important matters.

"Shoo!" "Go away, children!" "Don't bother the Teacher!" they said.

The children were surprised. The embarrassed parents pulled their children away and started to leave. Jesus was not happy that the disciples were sending the children away.

"Wait! Come back!" he called to the crowd of little ones. They obeyed, running back to the Savior's arms.

Then Jesus spoke firmly to his disciples. "Don't ever push the children away from me! They are very important. You should be just like a little child, if you want to understand my teaching."

The disciples learned a valuable lesson. And Jesus gave a special blessing to all the children who came to him.

God's Message

To understand
my kingdom
you must have the
faith of a little child.

Think simply
and believe.

Love me with
all your heart
and love others.

Then my kingdom
will be yours.

Chapter 26

The Hour of Darkness

*He said, "Father, if you are willing,
take this cup of suffering away from me.
But do what you want, not what I want."*

Luke 22:42

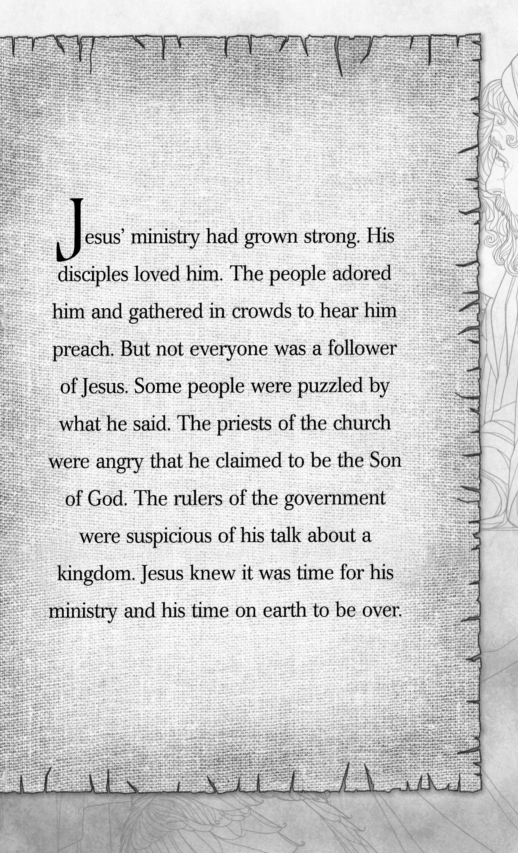

Jesus' ministry had grown strong. His disciples loved him. The people adored him and gathered in crowds to hear him preach. But not everyone was a follower of Jesus. Some people were puzzled by what he said. The priests of the church were angry that he claimed to be the Son of God. The rulers of the government were suspicious of his talk about a kingdom. Jesus knew it was time for his ministry and his time on earth to be over.

The Last Supper

Matthew 26:17–46; Mark 14:10–42; Luke 22:7–46; John 13:1–38

As Jesus and his twelve disciples sat around the table to share the Passover meal, Jesus told his friends this would be their last meal together and that a difficult time was coming.

Then he took a loaf of bread, blessed it, tore it in pieces, and shared it with everyone at the table. Jesus told them that the bread was like his own body that would be given for them. "Eat this to remember me," he said.

Jesus took a cup of wine, blessed it, and shared it with the disciples. "This cup of wine is a reminder of my promise to be your Savior," he said.

Then Jesus told them something that made them very sad. "One of you will turn against me and will give me to my enemies."

"Is it me?" each one asked.

"I would never do that," Peter protested.

Jesus said, "Peter, I'm sorry to tell you that, before morning, you will deny you know me—three times—before the rooster crows!"

Later than night Jesus walked to the Mount of Olives where there was a peaceful garden. He knelt down and prayed to his Father in heaven. He asked God to give him the courage to face the troubles ahead.

When his prayer time was over, Jesus rejoined the disciples. Suddenly a crowd of angry men showed up—the high priests, temple police, and leaders. One of Jesus' disciples, Judas, was with them. He walked over to Jesus and kissed him. (That was the signal to the leaders that Jesus was the one they wanted to arrest.) Judas was the traitor!

The temple police took Jesus away. The dark night and the dark times had begun.

God's Message

Lean on me, my Son.
I am with you.

Together, we will change
darkness to light
and sadness to joy.

You are the Savior
of my children.

Through you, our kingdom
will live forever.

Sneaky Schemes and a Disloyal Disciple

Matthew 26:69–75; Mark 14:66–72; Luke 22:55–62; John 18:16, 25–27

Rattling swords and marching feet broke the quiet in Jerusalem that night. Soldiers and temple leaders hustled Jesus through the dark, sleeping city.

Each time the group turned a corner, Peter darted behind a building. *What are these soldiers going to do to Jesus? Where are they taking my Lord? If they see me, will they arrest me too?* Peter wondered.

The soldiers pushed Jesus through the gate and into the courtyard of the house where the high priest waited for the prisoner. Peter slipped into the courtyard, close enough to watch and hear what was about to happen. He sat near the fire where others had gathered. He pulled his robe over his head, hoping no one would see his face.

A servant girl recognized Peter. "You're with him!" she said, pointing to Jesus.

"No, no. I don't even know that man," Peter lied.

The soldiers began to make fun of Jesus, hitting him and treating him badly.
A soldier sitting near Peter said, "Aren't you one of his disciples?"

Peter poked the fire with a stick and said, "I don't know what you're talking about."

The high priest began asking Jesus questions. Jesus answered, "Everything I've done has been out in the open for all to see. I've taught and ministered, but not in secret. Why are you treating me like this?"

Just then a soldier noticed Peter near the fire. "I saw you in the garden with Jesus! You are one of his disciples," he said.

Peter denied it. "Not me," he said. Then the courtyard rooster crowed his morning call. The sound of the rooster reminded Peter of Jesus' words. "You will deny me three times before the rooster crows."

Peter ran out of the courtyard. He cried and cried, disappointed with himself for not being true to Jesus.

God's Message

Darkness creeps
into every corner,
blocking out all light.

The things I said would
happen are coming true.

But trust in me.
I will never forsake you.

I am your Father
and you have my promise:
my light will shine again.

The Crucifixion

Matthew 27:27–56; Mark 15:16–41; Luke 23:26–49; John 19:17–30

People packed the streets of Jerusalem to look at Jesus. The word was all over town: Jesus had been condemned to die. He had been beaten, spit on, and made fun of. Now the soldiers whipped him, forcing him to march to the place where he would be executed.

Crowds of angry citizens who did not believe he was the son of God wanted him killed; followers of Jesus wanted him saved from the terrible punishment. Men shouted, women cried, children were puzzled by all the commotion.

In the middle of all the turmoil, Jesus trudged up the dusty road to the hill called Calvary. Without a word, the weary, beaten Savior struggled under the heavy wooden cross he was forced to carry.

The soldiers pounded huge nails through the hands and feet of Jesus and into the cross. They raised the cross, with Jesus on it, and stuck it in the ground. There Jesus hung for hours, in great pain. Two criminals hung on crosses next to him.

Many people made fun of Jesus as he suffered. "If he is the Son of God as he says, let him save himself," they laughed. One of the criminals made fun of him too. But the other criminal believed Jesus was God's Son. "When your kingdom comes, will you save me?" he asked Jesus. And Jesus promised to save him.

The painful punishment continued for hours. Jesus' mother and disciples watched, filled with sadness at his suffering. Soon the sun stopped shining. Darkness was all around. Then Jesus cried out, "It is finished." And he died.

Friends of Jesus took his body and buried it in a tomb. It was a sad time for the disciples. They cried for him and prayed together. But Jesus had one more amazing miracle to accomplish.

God's Message

Jesus has finished
his task here on earth;
to die for the sins
of all people.

Through tears,
friends and family
will reflect on his life.

But soon joyful
sounds of triumph
will fill the air.

Death has no power
over my Son.

The best is yet to come!

Chapter 27

The Resurrection

The angel said to the women, "Don't be afraid.
I know that you are looking for Jesus, who was crucified.
He is not here! He has risen, just as he said he would!
Come and see the place where he was lying."

Matthew 28:5–6

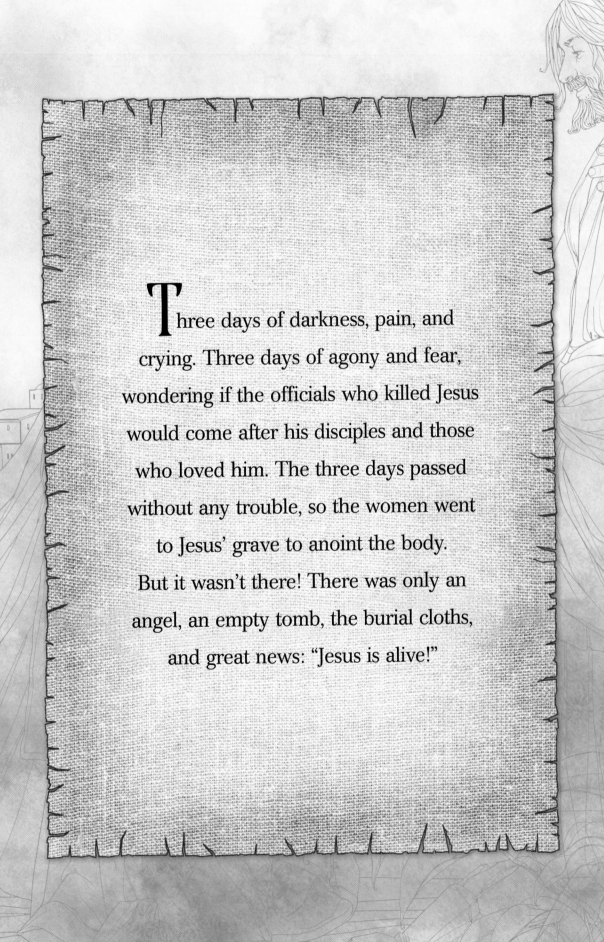

Three days of darkness, pain, and crying. Three days of agony and fear, wondering if the officials who killed Jesus would come after his disciples and those who loved him. The three days passed without any trouble, so the women went to Jesus' grave to anoint the body. But it wasn't there! There was only an angel, an empty tomb, the burial cloths, and great news: "Jesus is alive!"

Angelic Encounter

Matt 28:1–10; Mark 16:1–11; Luke 24:1–12; John 20:1–18

Even in their sadness, the women who were Jesus' followers knew they had work to do. When someone died, the women poured good-smelling oils on the body and wrapped it in a nice burial cloth.

So Mary Magdalene, Salome, Joanna, and Mary, James' mother, headed for the tomb on Sunday morning to take care of Jesus' body. On the way, they began to talk about the tomb and what they would do when they arrived. "Who will roll away that big heavy stone for us?" one of the women asked.

But when they arrived, the stone had already been moved from the tomb's entrance. Mary Magdalene ran ahead and peeked inside.

"He's gone!" she shouted. "Our Lord is gone! Look—the burial garments are still here, neatly folded up!"

"Don't be afraid," spoke a calm, quiet voice from the tomb. Mary Magdalene looked again and saw an angel.

"I know you're looking for Jesus. He's not here. He was raised from the dead, just as he had promised. Now go and tell the others he is risen," the angel said.

Running back to the house where the disciples had gathered, the women couldn't wait to share the great news about the Savior. But on the way, the women encountered still another surprise: Jesus himself!

"Good morning," Jesus said as he smiled at his friends.

"Lord!" the women cried joyfully, dropping to their knees and worshiping the Son of God.

"Go tell the others I'll meet them in Galilee," Jesus said.

The women got up and did as Jesus instructed them. "The Lord is risen!" they said over and over again as they hurried to meet the disciples and share the amazing news.

God's Message

When my Son was born,
the angels sang a chorus
of glad tidings
to the world:
a Savior is born.

Now, he is re-born
and, once again,
an angel proclaims
the good news.

He is risen from the dead!

Share it with everyone!
Christ is risen!
Hallelujah!

Reunion with Jesus

John 20:19–31

It had been an upsetting few days. Jesus had been arrested, treated badly, and then crucified. The disciples were worried that the leaders might come after them next. They might be in trouble for believing in Jesus. They kept the doors locked so the soldiers and leaders couldn't get to them.

The disciples argued and discussed Mary Magdelene's remarkable news. "I saw Jesus raised from the dead!" she had told them over and over.

As they talked, Jesus suddenly appeared in the locked room. The disciples were shocked. The last time they had seen him, he was dead!

"Peace be to you," Jesus said. He showed them the nail scars on his hands. He showed them the side of his body that had been cut by the soldier's sword.

When the disciples realized the person in front of them really was Jesus, they were very happy! And Jesus was happy to be with his friends again. He gave them a special blessing and told them he had a big job for them to do.

"I want you to tell everyone about the blessing that I came to give: forgiveness and life eternal for everyone who believes in me. Soon the Father will send the Holy Spirit to help you and give you strength and power," Jesus explained.

Though the disciples didn't understand everything, they understood that Jesus had done what he said: he had died and was alive again. The disciples knew they had been chosen to do an important job.

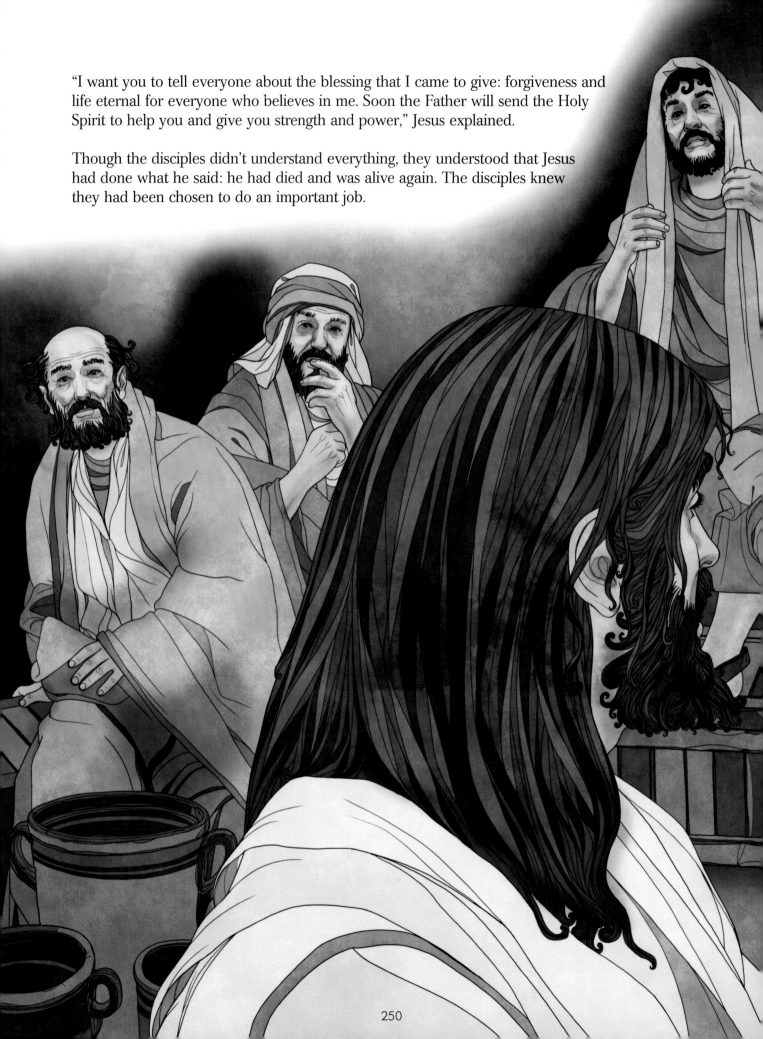

God's Message

My Son will soon leave the earth and return to heaven to be with me.

But in his place, I will send my Spirit to fill you with strength and power and the courage to tell everyone the good news that Jesus has saved the world.

Beach Breakfast

"I'm going fishing," Peter announced.

"Not without us!" the other disciples said. And off they went, dropping their nets in the water, hoping for a good catch. They worked all night long, but their nets came up empty. There was nothing to show for their night of work.

When the sun came up, a man on the shore called out to them, "Good morning! Did you catch anything for breakfast?"

"No," they grumbled, tired and hungry.

The man called again, "Throw the net on the right side of your boat and see what happens."

"Forget that. Let's go home," one said.

"Oh, one more try won't hurt," suggested another.

So they tried once more. Suddenly their net bulged with fish.

One disciple said to Peter, "Look, the man on the beach is Jesus!"

Peter was so excited to see Jesus again that he jumped in the water and swam to shore. The others rowed the boat carrying the big catch of fish. Jesus had already made a fire on the beach and was cooking breakfast for his friends.

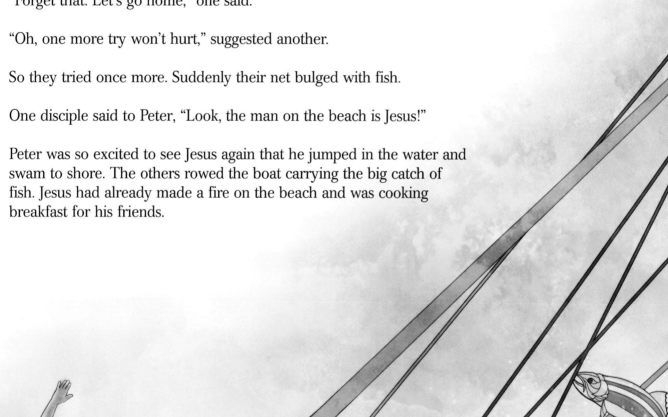

Later, Jesus spoke to Peter. "Peter, do you love me?"

Peter said, "You know that I love you."

Jesus said, "Peter, feed my lambs." He meant that Peter should teach the people about Jesus.

Jesus asked Peter the same question three times. Jesus wanted Peter to understand the important job he would have—to take care of the followers and teach them about the Son of God.

Finally the disciples understood that their job was to tell everyone the important news of Jesus' life, death, and his resurrection.

God's Message

One last time
my Son has come
to be with you.

Now you understand
what you must do.

Get ready to be filled
with my Spirit.

Leave your fishing nets
forever and go and become
fishers of men, telling people
all over the earth about
Jesus, my Son,
the Savior of the world!

Chapter 28

New Beginnings

*"But you will receive power when the
Holy Spirit comes on you. Then you will be
my witnesses in Jerusalem. You will be my witnesses
in all Judea and Samaria. And you will be my witnesses
from one end of the earth to the other."*

Acts 1:8

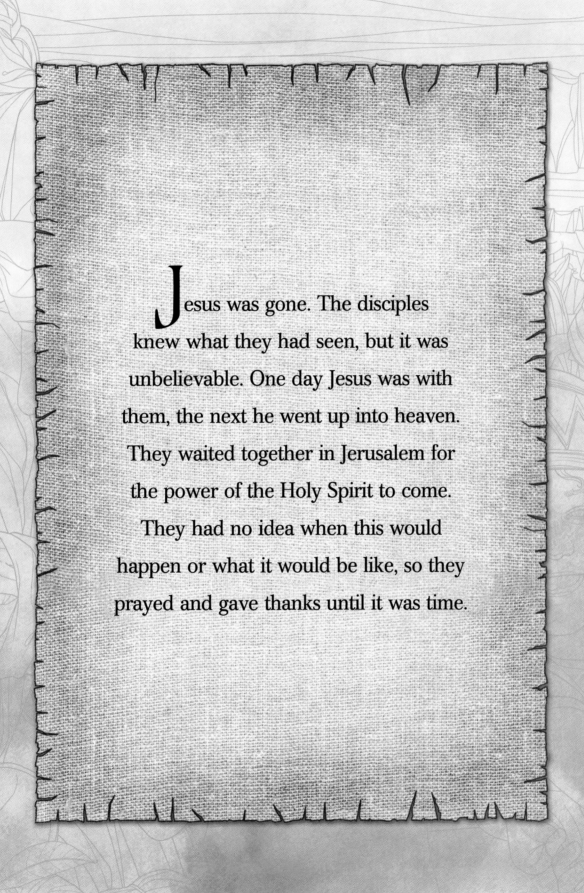

Jesus was gone. The disciples knew what they had seen, but it was unbelievable. One day Jesus was with them, the next he went up into heaven. They waited together in Jerusalem for the power of the Holy Spirit to come. They had no idea when this would happen or what it would be like, so they prayed and gave thanks until it was time.

About three thousand people heard the message and were baptized that day. The Pentecost event made the believers feel like family. Even though they came from different places, spoke different languages, and wore different clothes, they loved each other. They spent time together sharing meals and prayer time. They cared for each other in every way.

The Holy Spirit's presence encouraged the believers and the disciples. Since they wanted everyone to know about Jesus, they did all they could to share the good news.

God's Message

My Spirit dwells within you.

The Holy Spirit has come
just as I promised,
through my Son.

Let the Spirit's
comfort bring you peace.

Let the Spirit's power
fill you with courage.

Perform miracles
in my name.

Tell the world that
the Messiah has come.

Saul Meets His Match

Acts 9:1–19

While the disciples and new believers, known as Christians, were spreading the good news about Jesus, a man named Saul was trying to stop them. Saul didn't believe in Jesus, and he didn't like any of the people who did. He traveled from town to town hunting the Christians, arresting them, and dragging them off to jail. The believers were terrified of Saul.

God decided to show Saul his power and make a believer out of him. As Saul and his helpers traveled to the city of Damascus, a bright light flashed, knocking Saul to the ground. He heard a voice saying, "Saul, Saul, why are you being so cruel to me?"

"Who-o-o are you?" Saul cried out, shielding his eyes.

"I am Jesus, the one you are trying to hurt. Now go into the city, and you will be told what you must do."

As Saul struggled to his feet, he opened his eyes … but he was blind! The helpers led Saul by the hand and went to an inn in Damascus. Saul stayed there by himself. He prayed, trying to imagine what Jesus would want of him.

Soon God sent a man named Ananias to speak to Saul. Even though Ananias was afraid of Saul, he did exactly what God had instructed him to do.

Ananias entered Saul's room and spoke. "Saul, the Lord sent me here. He is the same one who appeared to you on the road. He wants you to be able to see again and to be filled with the Holy Spirit." Ananias placed his hands on Saul's face. Immediately scaly scabs fell off Saul's eyes and he could see again!

Ananias taught Saul everything about Jesus. Saul was baptized. He changed his name to Paul. He met other disciples in the area and came to understand the message of Jesus. Paul loved the people he once hated—he saw them with new eyes, all because God had chosen him.

God's Message

I have chosen you
to follow me.

You have been
changed and are
ready to do my work.

Go out with great joy
and spread the good news.

Chapter 29

Paul's Mission

So you must go and make disciples of all nations.
Baptize them in the name of the
Father and of the Son and of the Holy Spirit.

Matthew 28:19

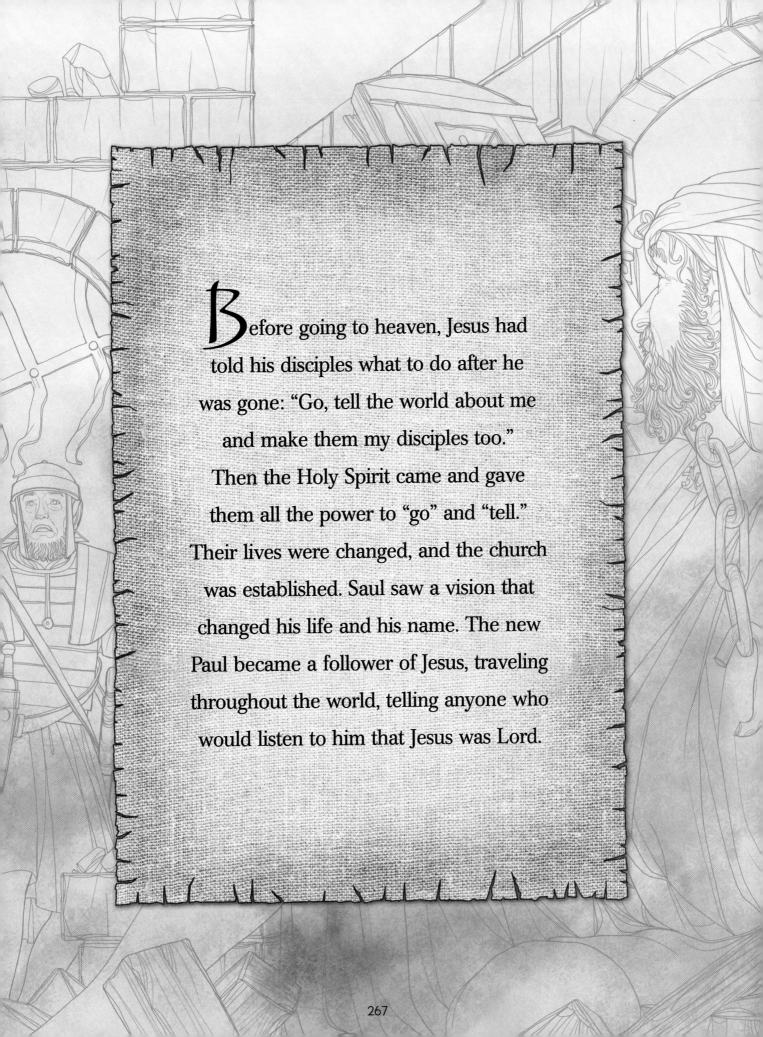

Before going to heaven, Jesus had told his disciples what to do after he was gone: "Go, tell the world about me and make them my disciples too." Then the Holy Spirit came and gave them all the power to "go" and "tell." Their lives were changed, and the church was established. Saul saw a vision that changed his life and his name. The new Paul became a follower of Jesus, traveling throughout the world, telling anyone who would listen to him that Jesus was Lord.

Paul and Silas in Prison

Acts 16:16–40

Paul traveled from town to town, but now, instead of hurting believers, he encouraged and taught them. On one particular journey, he and his companion, Silas, were constantly followed by a slave girl who had an evil spirit in her. This spirit gave the girl the power to tell people what would happen in the future. People paid the slave-girl's owners for this knowledge.

Paul and Silas could hardly do their ministry because the slave-girl kept shouting and interrupting them everywhere they went.

After a few days of this behavior, Paul decided he had to do something. He turned to the girl and shouted, "In the name of Jesus Christ, I command you to leave her!" The evil spirit left the girl immediately.

Paul had done a wonderful thing, but the slave-girl's owners were mad. Now the girl couldn't earn money for them. They took out their anger on Paul and Silas. They dragged them to the authorities of the city who arrested them, beat them up, and threw them in jail.

Being in jail didn't stop Paul and Silas from praising God. They loudly sang praise songs while the other prisoners looked on, surprised at their joyful attitude.

As they sang, a huge earthquake rattled and shook the jail. All the doors of the jail flew open; the chains fell off the prisoners. The jailer was startled to find Paul and Silas still in the jail when they could have run away. He knew that Paul and Silas worshiped the one true God. "What do I have to do to be saved?" he asked.

Paul answered, "Believe in the Lord Jesus, and you will be saved."

The jailer took Paul and Silas to his home, where they shared the good news of Jesus with the jailer's family. Then the jailer and his family were baptized.

God's Message

I am always with you:
on the streets of a city,
in a ship heading
out to sea,
even in a jail cell.

I will take care of you
and watch over you.

Powerful and wonderful
things will happen
when you follow me
and do my will.

Paul's Teachings and Writings

1 Corinthians 12–13; Ephesians 2; Philippians 1

For the rest of his life, Paul devoted himself to preaching about Jesus and his resurrection. He started churches in many towns and tried to revisit them when he could. But there were so many churches in so many towns, so Paul wrote letters to the new believers to help them live like Jesus. These letters were full of important, encouraging words about God's love.

To the church of God in Corinth Paul wrote: "I want to share with you the most excellent way to love."

God's Message

Suppose I speak in the languages
of human beings and of angels.
If I don't have love,
I am only a loud gong or a noisy cymbal.

Suppose I have the gift of prophecy.
Suppose I can understand all the secret things
of God and know everything about him.
And suppose I have enough faith to move mountains.
If I don't have love, I am nothing at all.

Suppose I give everything I have to poor people.
And suppose I give my body to be burned.
If I don't have love, I get nothing at all.

Love is patient. Love is kind.
It does not want what belongs to others.

It does not brag. It is not proud. It is not rude.
It does not look out for its own interests.

It does not easily become angry.
It does not keep track of other people's wrongs.

Love is not happy with evil.
But it is full of joy when the truth is spoken.

It always protects. It always trusts.
It always hopes. It never gives up.

The three most important things to have
are faith, hope, and love.
But the greatest of them is love.

You have instructed
my people well.

Many people and
many families
will read your words
and will be touched
by my Spirit.

They will come to
know me in their hearts
and, like you, they
will be transformed.

Chapter 30

Paul's Final Days

I have fought the good fight.
I have finished the race.
I have kept the faith.

2 Timothy 4:7

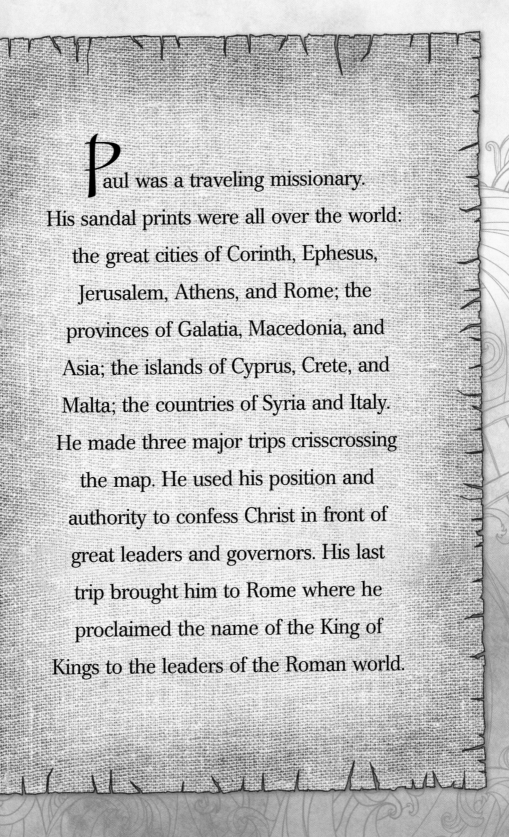

Paul was a traveling missionary.
His sandal prints were all over the world:
the great cities of Corinth, Ephesus,
Jerusalem, Athens, and Rome; the
provinces of Galatia, Macedonia, and
Asia; the islands of Cyprus, Crete, and
Malta; the countries of Syria and Italy.
He made three major trips crisscrossing
the map. He used his position and
authority to confess Christ in front of
great leaders and governors. His last
trip brought him to Rome where he
proclaimed the name of the King of
Kings to the leaders of the Roman world.

Shipwrecked!

Acts 27–28

Paul never made it a secret that he followed Jesus. He preached in public, where anyone could hear his message. The Jewish leaders tried to find ways to quiet him, and finally he was arrested and sent to trial.

Paul demanded they send him to Rome. He was born a Roman, and that gave him some special privileges. One privilege was that he could plead his case before Caesar, the Roman Emperor.

So began a long journey to Rome by ship, through the Mediterranean Sea. Paul warned the captain, "It's not a good idea to sail now—we should wait for better weather." But the captain didn't listen to Paul. Soon a great storm kicked up the waves, tossing the ship to and fro.

For days the storm battered the boat, frightening the crew and the other prisoners on board. The captain ordered the sailors to toss the cargo overboard to lighten the ship.

While everyone else was frightened and worried, Paul stood up and shouted over the crashing waves, "Everything's going to be all right! No one will drown, but this ship will break up. God sent an angel to me last night who told me, 'Don't give up, Paul. You and everyone on this ship will make it to shore.' So, dear friends, be strong! God will do exactly what he told me."

Several days later the ship broke up on a sandbar, and everyone swam to shore. They were all safe, just as God had promised.

God's Message

Do not be afraid,
my children.

I will be with you,
always and forever.

I have a plan for you—
a great and grand
and glorious vision
for your future.

Trust in me.
I am your Father.

Chapter 31

Revelation

"Look! I am coming soon!"

Revelation 22:7

While on earth, Jesus assured his disciples that he would come back to earth again. For many years, the people who believed in Jesus thought his return would happen soon. But it never did. And now, thousands of years later, we are still waiting for God to fulfill this promise. This glorious event is worth waiting for. We live in hope of its coming. We live in joy waiting for Christ's spectacular coming to earth again.

Jesus Is Coming Again

Revelation 21–22

Sent away to an island for the rest of his life, Jesus' friend John was given visions of heaven to share so the churches would stay strong and true to their faith in Jesus. The apostle John wrote down everything he saw.

John wrote that someday Jesus will return and heaven will be the new home for people who believe in him. On that day, everyone will see a beautiful new heaven and new earth. The Holy City of Jerusalem will be a golden city shining with God's glory like a brilliant jewel. A silvery clear river flowing with the water of life will stream down from God's holy throne through the city street. The great tree of life from the Garden of Eden will grow in the center of the city. Each month, the tree will grow a different fruit and its leaves will be used for healing. The twelve city gates will stay wide open all the time with an angel at each gate.

Jesus will be like a king sitting on a royal throne. A voice from the throne will announce, "Now God will dwell with humans and he will live with them. They will be his people, and he will be their God. There will be no more tears, no more death or crying or pain, because the old things are gone forever."

The day Jesus returns will be the most wonderful and glorious day ever. Greater than any earthly celebration we know of or can imagine. We will sing and shout praises. We will live with God forever!

God's Message

Wait patiently, my children,
for I will come again.

I will remember
my promise and
my kingdom will come.

On that day,
there will be singing
in the streets and
rejoicing in heaven.

Peace and joy
and goodness will replace
war, sadness, and evil.

Sin and death
will be forgotten.
All will be well.

And the King of Kings
and Lord of Lords
will reign on his throne
forever and ever.

Acknowledgements

A beautiful Bible storybook requires an army of creative minds.

We are deeply grateful for the forces behind this book, including:

Fausto Bianchi, for your unforgettable artistry.

Steve James, for your amazing color work.

The Zondervan team, for your careful shepherding of this book.

Family Minister Selma Rivas, for your remarkable insight.

Janie Padilla, for your quiet service and valuable assistance.

Steve and Cheryl Green, for your steady counsel and faithful friendship.

To the children in our lives who inspire us daily.

And to the Writer of the Word.

Thank you for the honor of telling your stories to a new generation.